Good Morning
REVOLUTION

A world I dream where black or white,
Whatever race you be,
Will *share* the bounties of the earth
And every man is free.

      —Langston Hughes

Good Morning
REVOLUTION
Uncollected Social Protest
Writings by

LANGSTON HUGHES

Edited and

with an introduction by

FAITH BERRY

Foreword by

Saunders Redding

LAWRENCE HILL & COMPANY

WESTPORT

Library of Congress
Cataloging in Publication Data
Hughes, Langston, 1902-1967.
Good morning, revolution.
I. Title.
PS3515.U274G6 1973   818′.5′209   73-81747
ISBN 0-88208-023-7
ISBN 0-88208-024-5 (pbk.)

ISBN clothbound edition 0-88208-023-7
ISBN paperback edition 0-88208-024-5

Library of Congress catalogue card number: 73-81747

First edition November 1973
Lawrence Hill & Company, Publishers, Inc.
Manufactured in the United States of America
3 4 5 6 7 8 9 10 11 12
Design by Andrea Marquez

Contents

Acknowledgments

For materials and helpful assistance during research for this book, grateful acknowledgment is extended to the Library of Congress; Moorland-Spingarn Collection, Howard University Library; The Schomburg Collection, New York Public Library; The Bancroft Library, University of California, Berkeley; the American Institute of Marxist Studies; and the Library and Museum of the Performing Arts, New York Public Library.

I am grateful to my mother and father, J. M. and T. M. Berry, and to my sister and brother-in-law, Gail and Togo West, for help in many ways during my work on this project.

I also wish to thank Saunders Redding for his encouragement and foreword.

Acknowledgments

FOREWORD

This collection of prose peices and poems by Langston Hughes has an important purpose—to reestablish firmly and irrevocably a dimension to the genius of Hughes that well-meaning critics and literary historians have ignored (or been ignorant of), blurred, or purposefully eroded. Hughes certainly deserves the regard in which he is held as an Afro-American poet and writer. From the 1920s until his death in 1967, no poet caught with such sharp immediacy and intensity the humor and the pathos, the irony and the humiliation, the beauty and the bitterness of the experience of being Negro in America; and I think it should be added that no one contributed more to the current refunding of Negro folk material and the reshaping of Negro legend. But there is another dimension. Hughes was a revolutionary writer and poet. If, heretofore, the fact has not been operative in the making of his reputation, it is in part Hughes's own fault. That was the way he wanted it. Why he wanted it that way is made clear in the introduction to this volume and will be thoroughly explicated in the Hughes biography Faith Berry is presently completing. Not having the benefit of Miss Berry's painstaking research. I can only mention the matter here by way of two anecdotes.

Back in the late 1940s and early 1950s, when I was in charge of the lecture series at Hampton Institute, Langston Hughes accepted an invitation to read his poetry. As a reader of his own poetry, he was no Dylan Thomas, and his extemporaneous comments on the origin, the inspiration, and the meaning of the various pieces he read were the best part of the program. When he asked my opinion, I told him exactly that, and went on to remark that he had not included any of those poems that had always struck me as most expressive and most representative of him as "poet-spokesman" (as he was frequently characterized) and as reflective of his individual emotional experiences. Nor did he read even a single one of the very moving militant pieces that carried broad socio-political implications.

Some years later, in 1962, Langston and I were invited to participate in a week-long "All-African Writers Conference" in Kampala, Uganda. I suppose my invitation was initiated by the fact that I was connected with the bi-racial American Society for African Culture (now defunct), under the auspices of which I was lecturing in Africa that year. Langston, of course, was well known and greatly admired there, where his poems, and especially those in his "African" canon, were widely read. At any rate, we both attended, and Hughes, asked to give a reading, again stuck to his conventional verses on conventional themes. Later that night a half dozen African writers and poets, including Wole Soyinka, James Ngugi, Birago Diop, Bloke Modisani and Ezekiel Mphahlele, had Langston and me join a bull session, during the lengthy course of which the subject of Langston's revolutionary poems came up. Why had he not read any of them? He said he thought those particular poems were inappropriate for the occasion. This was the third night, and what the conference had developed into by then was a heated colloquy on the revolution against the imposition of Western cultural, political and artistic standards upon the black peoples of the world. When this was pointed out, Langston lapsed into silence.

Now Miss Berry has brought together the pieces that Langston Hughes hesitated to read and discuss publicly—although some of them were written as late as 1957—during the last years of his life. In bringing them together, Miss Berry has performed an important service to American literary history and criticism. She realizes that these militant, revolutionary pieces give expression to a vaunted, though still unattained, American ideal, and that their emotive characteristics communicate the wish, the hope, and the faith that were Langston Hughes's all along, and that, indeed, inspired and were the themes of nearly all he wrote— ". . . nary a sign of a color line/For the Freedom Train will be yours and mine!"

Saunders Redding

INTRODUCTION

> After a man's long work is over
> and the sound of his voice is still,
> those in whose regard he has held a
> high place find his image strangely
> simplified and summarized.
>
> —Henry James

Langston Hughes was best known as a folk poet, pursuing the theme "I, too, sing America." But that image, which he accepted though did not choose, is only part of his legacy. During a career which covered four decades, in which he tried every literary genre, he wrote some of the most revolutionary works by any American writer of his generation. He was called the "poet laureate of the Negro race," but never for reasons which included his most radical verse. Editors, publishers and critics who hailed him as "poet laureate" ignored that part of his canon which did not fit his popular image. Seen from their perspective, his revolutionary prose and poetry represented an aberration, an isolated phase of his early career.

Such writings were not a product only of his early career, as the pieces in this volume attest. Many had appeared in print by 1940, by which time he was the established author of seven poetry collections, a novel, a juvenile, a volume of short stories, a Broadway play, an autobiography, and the recipient of numerous literary prizes. Some of his most radical works were written during the same period when his popular works appeared, a fact overlooked by those who attributed his revolutionary writing to a passing phase. The "phase" actually lasted as long as he lived.

In order to satisfy his public, his critics, his publishers and himself, he faced an ongoing inner struggle between what he wanted to write and what his audience expected him to write, between his public image and private self, between his performance and his integrity. Publishers who were enthusiastic about his jazz and blues poems would not touch poems such as "Good Morning Revolution." He could write revolutionary tracts, but he could not make a living from them, a situation that continually posed for him the choice between making a livelihood—and writing was his livelihood—or a sacrifice. Not to compromise his principles, he contributed some of the most incisive works he ever produced to small, obscure magazines and newspapers. This volume contains those militant, revolutionary pieces of social protest written over a thirty-two year period. It also contains several works heretofore unpublished.

Hughes's most outspoken prose and poetry is from the 1930s. This was a period when many American artists and writers, concerned about the economic depression in America and the rise of Fascism in Europe and disillusioned by the values of capitalist society as a whole, were moving toward the left. Hughes's revolutionary writing of that decade was a result not only of those forces but of his travels to Russia, China and Spain, all of which are reflected in this volume. The social and political ideas he espoused during the 1930s are evident in his poetry as early as 1925. They appear in his later writings, though he was by then reluctant to discuss such ideas publicly, especially on lecture tours. In the 1940s and thereafter, his income was as dependent upon public readings as upon published books, a major reason he did not anthologize works he was hesitant to read before an audience. Late in his career he attempted to publish a volume which eventually appeared posthumously as *The Panther and the Lash* (1967). The only other collections of radical verse he ever issued were two brief pamphlets during the 1930s: *Scottsboro Limited* (1932) and *A New Song* (1938), the former contributed to raise funds for the defense in the Scottsboro Case, and the latter to a literary series published by the International Workers Order, a left-wing fraternal organization.

The events of the 1950s, however, reveal the most far-reaching answer to why he never anthologized some of the selections in this book. As a result of the political stance taken earlier in his career, most notably toward the Soviet Union, he was a target of the ominous "cold war" crusade better known as McCarthyism. During that era of unparalleled political paranoia, when anyone who ever had expressed praise of Russia was branded a public enemy and treated as such, Hughes found his reputation threatened and his career at stake. In March 1953, summoned to testify before Joseph McCarthy's Senate Committee on Government Operations, he was pressed to answer such questions as "Would you tell this committee frankly as to whether or not there was ever a period of time in your life when you believed in the Soviet form of government?"

Hughes was never a member of the Communist party, though indeed he once had been sympathetic to it, a fact he did not deny (without apologizing) during the McCarthy hearings. The emergence of McCarthyism meant "black lists" in the publishing world, the power to destroy careers at apogee. As a result of the McCarthy hearings, for several years, Hughes's name was on a list of "un-American" authors whose books were banned from U.S.I.A. libraries throughout the world. His books were also banned from the schools and libraries of certain states that passed anti-Communist laws. An influential lecture bureau, which long had scheduled his speaking engagements, canceled his contract. His public appearances often were met with pickets carrying signs with the words "traitor," "red," and "Communist sympathizer."

In those years before a *détente* in US-Sino-Soviet relations— paradoxically reached through an American President whose early political career was devoted to McCarthyism—Hughes suffered the consequences of being ahead of his time, ready for America before America was ready for him. He died leaving some of his most forthright statements about Russia and China out of circulation, for fear they would be misunderstood. His second autobiographical volume, *I Wonder As I Wander* (1956), fully presents his experiences during a journey to both those countries, but not his political attitudes. Certain related selections in this volume have been inaccessible for more than forty years. It should be noted that their publication now, only a brief time after amicable overtures by Washington to the USSR and the People's Republic of China, is purely coincidental to diplomatic events. The collection was not prepared to follow in the footsteps of official political policy, a pattern often obvious in American cultural and artistic endeavors.

The works were collected as evidence of some of the best

writing ever done by Langston Hughes, whose full canon, rather than a selective part, merits wide recognition and understanding.

—Faith Berry
July, 1973

1
REVOLUTION

LETTER TO THE ACADEMY

The gentlemen who have got to be classics and are now old
    with beards (or dead and in their graves) will kindly
    come forward and speak upon the subject

Of the Revolution. I mean the gentlemen who wrote lovely
    books about the defeat of the flesh and the triumph of
    the spirit that sold in the hundreds of thousands and
    are studied in the high schools and read by the best
    people will kindly come forward and

Speak about the Revolution—where the flesh triumphs (as
    well as the spirit) and the hungry belly eats, and there
    are no best people, and the poor are mighty and no
    longer poor, and the young by the hundreds of
    thousands are free from hunger to grow and study and
    love and propagate, bodies and souls unchained
    without My Lord saying a commoner shall never
    marry my daughter or the Rabbi crying cursed be the
    mating of Jews and Gentiles or Kipling writing never
    the twain shall meet—

For the twain have met. But please—all you gentlemen with
    beards who are so wise and old and who write better
    than we do and whose souls have triumphed (in spite
    of hungers and wars and the evils about you) and
    whose books have soared in calmness and beauty aloof
    from the struggle to the library shelves and the desks
    of students and who are now classics—come forward
    and speak upon

The subject of the Revolution.

We want to know what in the hell you'd say?

                                            Moscow, 1933

International Literature, No. 5, 1933

GOOD MORNING, REVOLUTION

Good morning, Revolution:
        You're the very best friend
        I ever had.
We gonna pal around together from now on.
Say, listen, Revolution:

You know, the boss where I used to work,
The guy that gimme the air to cut down expenses,
He wrote a long letter to the papers about you:
Said you was a trouble maker, a alien-enemy,
In other words a son-of-a-bitch.
He called up the police
And told 'em to watch out for a guy
Named Revolution.

You see,
The boss knows you're my friend.
He sees us hangin' out together.
He knows we're hungry, and ragged,
And ain't got a damn thing in this world—
And are gonna do something about it.

The boss's got all he needs, certainly,
        Eats swell,
        Owns a lotta houses,
        Goes vacationin',
        Breaks strikes,
        Runs politics, bribes police,
        Pays off congress,
        And struts all over the earth—

But me, I ain't never had enough to eat.
Me, I ain't never been warm in winter.
Me, I ain't never known security—
All my life, been livin' hand to mouth,
        Hand to mouth.

Listen, Revolution,
        We're buddies, see—
        Together,
        We can take everything:
        Factories, arsenals, houses, ships,
        Railroads, forests, fields, orchards,
        Bus lines, telegraphs, radiòs,
         (Jesus! Raise hell with radios!)
        Steel mills, coal mines, oil wells, gas,
        All the tools of production,
         (Great day in the morning!)
        Everything—
        And turn 'em over to the people who work.
        Rule and run 'em for us people who work.

Boy! Them radios—
Broadcasting that very first **morning** to USSR:
Another member the International Soviet's done come
Greetings to the Socialist Soviet Republics
Hey you rising workers everywhere greetings
>And we'll sign it: Germany
>Sign it: China
>Sign it: Africa
>Sign it: Poland
>Sign it: Italy
>Sign it: America
>Sign it with my one name: Worker
On that day when no one will be hungry, cold, oppressed,
Anywhere in the world again.

>That's our job!

>I been starvin' too long,
>Ain't you?

>Let's go, Revolution!.

New Masses, **September 1932**

WHITE MAN

Sure, I know you!
You're a White Man.
I'm a Negro.
You take all the best jobs
And leave us the garbage cans to empty and
The halls to clean.
You have a good time in a big house at
Palm Beach
And rent us the back alleys
And the dirty slums.
You enjoy Rome—
And *take* Ethiopia.
White Man! White Man!
Let Louis Armstrong play it—
And you copyright it
And make the money.
You're the smart guy, White Man!
You got everything!
But now,
I hear your name ain't really White Man.

I hear it's something
Marx wrote down
Fifty years ago—
That rich people don't like to read.
Is that true, White Man?
Is your name in a book
Called The Communist Manifesto?
Is your name spelled
C-A-P-I-T-A-L-I-S-T?
Are you always a White Man?
Huh?

New Masses, December 15, 1936

REVOLUTION

Great Mob that knows no fear—
Come here!
And raise your hand
Against this man
Of iron and steel and gold
Who's bought and sold
You—
Each one—
For the last thousand years.
Come here,
Great mob that knows no fear,
And tear him limb from limb,
Split his golden throat
Ear to ear,
And end his time forever,
Now—
This year—
Great mob that knows no fear.

New Masses, February 20, 1934

2
MEMO TO NON-WHITE PEOPLES

The Same

It is the same everywhere for me:
On the docks at Sierra Leone,
In the cotton fields of Alabama,
In the diamond mines of Kimberley,
On the coffee hills of Haiti,
The banana lands of Central America,
The streets of Harlem,
And the cities of Morocco and Tripoli.

Black:
Exploited, beaten, and robbed,
Shot and killed.
Blood running into

> DOLLARS
> POUNDS
> FRANCS
> PESETAS
> LIRE

For the wealth of the exploiters—
Blood that never comes back to me again.
Better that my blood
Runs into the deep channels of Revolution,
Runs into the strong hands of Revolution,
Stains all flags red,
Drives me away from

> SIERRA LEONE
> KIMBERLEY
> ALABAMA
> HAITI
> CENTRAL AMERICA
> HARLEM
> MOROCCO
> TRIPOLI

And all the black lands everywhere.
The force that kills,
The power that robs,
And the greed that does not care.
Better that my blood makes one with the blood

Of all the struggling workers in the world—
Till every land is free of

> DOLLAR ROBBERS
> POUND ROBBERS
> FRANC ROBBERS
> PESETA ROBBERS
> LIRE ROBBERS
> LIFE ROBBERS—

Until the Red Armies of the International Proletariat
Their faces, black, white, olive, yellow, brown,
Unite to raise the blood-red flag that
Never will come down!

The Negro Worker, September/October 1932

THE ENGLISH

In ships all over the world
The English comb their hair for dinner,
Stand watch on the bridge,
Guide by strange stars,
Take on passengers,
Slip up hot rivers,
Nose across lagoons,
Bargain for trade,
Buy, sell or rob,
Load oil, load fruit,
Load cocoa beans, load gold.
In ships all over the world,
Comb their hair for dinner.

The Crisis, July 1930

JOHANNESBURG MINES

In the Johannesburg mines
There are 240,000 natives working.

What kind of poem
Would you make out of that?

240,000 natives working
In the Johannesburg mines.

The Crisis, February 1928

Black Workers

The bees work.
Their work is taken from them.
We are like the bees—
But it won't last
Forever.

The Crisis, April 1933

Cubes

In the days of the broken cubes of Picasso
And in the days of the broken songs of the
Young men
A little too drunk to sing
And the young women
A little too unsure of love to love—
I met on the boulevards of Paris
An African from Senegal.

God
Knows why the French
Amuse themselves bringing to Paris
Negroes from Senegal.

It's the old game of the boss and the bossed,
    boss and the bossed,
Amused
    and
Amusing,
    worked and working
Behind the cubes of black and white,
        black and white,
    black and white

But since it is the old game,
For fun
They give him the three old prostitutes of
    France—
Liberty, Egality, Fraternity—
And all three of 'em sick
In spite of the tax to the government
And the legal houses
And the doctors
And the *Marseillaise.*

Of course, the young African from Senegal
Carries back from Paris
A little more disease
To spread among the black girls in the palm
    huts.
He brings them as a gift
    disease—
From light to darkness
        disease—
From the boss to the bossed
            disease—
From the game of black and white
    disease
From the city of the broken cubes of Picasso

                        d
                          i
              s
        e
              a
                  s
                e

New Masses, March 13, 1934

BLACK SEED

World-wide dusk
    Of dear dark faces
Driven before an alien wind,
Scattered like seed
From far-off places
Growing in soil
That's strange and thin,
Hybrid plants
In another's garden,
Flowers
In a land
That's not your own,
Cut by the shears
Of the white-faced gardeners—

Tell them to leave you alone!

Opportunity, December 1930

White Shadows

I'm looking for a house
In the world
Where white shadows
Will not fall.

There is no such house,
Dark brother,
No such house
At all.

Contempo, September 15, 1931

Envoy to Africa

My name is Lord Piggly-Wiggly
    Wogglesfoot Brown.
I was born in a quaint old English
    manor town.
I now find myself engaged in a
    diplomatic chore
That looks as though it might turn
    into a bit of a bore.
I was sent to inform the natives of
    this dark place
That the Atlantic Charter will eventually
    apply to their race.
Of course, at the moment, we could
    hardly afford
To stretch the Atlantic Charter that
    broad.
But I will say this to each native
    race:
      Some day you'll be equal—
      If you'll just stay in your place.

The Crisis, April 1953

Memo to Non-White Peoples

They will let you have dope
Because they are quite willing
To drug you or kill you.

They will let you have babies
Because they are quite willing
To pauperize you—
Or use your kids as labor boys
For army, air force, or uranium mine.

They will let you have alcohol
To make you sodden and drunk
And foolish.

They will gleefully let you
Kill your damn self any way you choose
With liquor, drugs, or whatever.

It's the same from Cairo to Chicago,
Cape Town to the Caribbean,
Do you travel the Stork Club circuit
To dear old Shepherd's Hotel?
 (Somebody burnt Shepherd's up.)
I'm sorry but it is
The same from Cairo to Chicago,
Cape Town to the Carib Hilton,
Exactly the same.

Africa South, April/June 1957

To Certain Negro Leaders

Voices crying in the wilderness,
At so much per word
From the white folks:
"Be meek and humble,
All you niggers,
And do not cry
Too loud."

New Masses, February 1931

Sunset in Dixie

The sun
Is gonna go down
In Dixie
Some of these days
With such a splash
That everybody who ever knew
What yesterday was
Is gonna forget—
When that sun
Goes down in Dixie.

The Crisis, September 1941

3
THE RICH AND
THE POOR

Rising Waters

To you
Who are the
Foam on the sea
And not the sea—
What of the jagged rocks,
And the waves themselves,
And the force of the mounting waters?
You are
But foam on the sea,
You rich ones—
Not the sea.

The Workers Monthly, April 1925

Advertisement for the Waldorf-Astoria

Fine living à la carte!

LISTEN, HUNGRY ONES!

Look! See what *Vanity Fair* says about the
    new Waldorf-Astoria:
    "All the luxuries of private home. . . ."
Now, won't that be charming when the last flophouse
    has turned you down this winter?
    Furthermore:
"It is far beyond anything hitherto attempted in the hotel
    world. . . ." It cost twenty-eight million dollars. The fa-
    mous Oscar Tschirky is in charge of banqueting.
    Alexandre Gastaud is chef. It will be a distinguished
    background for society.
So when you've got no place else to go, homeless and hungry
    ones, choose the Waldorf as a background for your rags—
(Or do you still consider the subway after midnight good
    enough?)

ROOMERS

Take a room at the new Waldorf, you down-and-outers—
    sleepers in charity's flop-houses where God pulls a
    long face, and you have to pray to get a bed.
They serve swell board at the Waldorf-Astoria. Look at this
menu, will you:

GUMBO CREOLE
CRABMEAT IN CASSOLETTE
BOILED BRISKET OF BEEF
SMALL ONIONS IN CREAM
WATERCRESS SALAD
PEACH MELBA

Have luncheon there this afternoon, all you jobless.
    Why not?
Dine with some of the men and women who got rich off of
    your labor, who clip coupons with clean white fingers
    because your hands dug coal, drilled stone, sewed gar-
    ments, poured steel to let other people draw dividends
    and live easy.
(Or haven't you had enough yet of the soup-lines and the bit-
    ter bread of charity?)
Walk through Peacock Alley tonight before dinner, and get
    warm, anyway. You've got nothing else to do.

EVICTED FAMILIES

All you families put out in the street:
    Apartments in the Towers are only $10,000 a year.
    (Three rooms and two baths.) Move in there until
    times get good, and you can do better. $10,000 and $1.00
    are about the same to you, aren't they?
Who cares about money with a wife and kids homeless, and
    nobody in the family working? Wouldn't a duplex
    high above the street be grand, with a view of the rich-
    est city in the world at your nose?"
"A lease, if you prefer, or an arrangement terminable at will."

NEGROES

Oh, Lawd, I done forgot Harlem!
Say, you colored folks, hungry a long time in 135th Street—
    they got swell music at the Waldorf-Astoria. It sure is a
    mighty nice place to shake hips in, too. There's danc-
    ing after supper in a big warm room. It's cold as hell
    on Lenox Avenue. All you've had all day is a cup of
    coffee. Your pawnshop overcoat's a ragged banner on
    your hungry frame. You know, downtown folks are just
    crazy about Paul Robeson! Maybe they'll like you, too,
    black mob from Harlem. Drop in at the Waldorf this
    afternoon for tea. Stay to dinner. Give Park Avenue a
    lot of darkie color—free for nothing! Ask the Junior

Leaguers to sing a spiritual for you. They probably
know 'em better than you do—and their lips won't be
so chapped with cold after they step out of their closed
cars in the undercover driveways.

Hallelujah! Undercover driveways!
Ma soul's a witness for de Waldorf-Astoria!

(A thousand nigger section-hands keep the roadbeds smooth,
so investments in railroads pay ladies with diamond
necklaces staring at Cert murals.)

Thank God A-mighty!

(And a million niggers bend their backs on rubber planta-
tions, for rich behinds to ride on thick tires to the
Theatre Guild tonight.)

Ma soul's a witness!

(And here we stand, shivering in the cold, in Harlem.)

Glory be to God—
De Waldorf-Astoria's open!

EVERYBODY

So get proud and rare back; everybody! The new Waldorf-As-
toria's open!

(Special siding for private cars from the railroad yards.)

You ain't been there yet?

(A thousand miles of carpet and a million bathrooms.)

What's the matter?

You haven't seen the ads in the papers? Didn't you get a card?
Don't you know they specialize in American cooking?
Ankle on down to 49th Street at Park Avenue. Get up
off that subway bench tonight with the evening *POST*
for cover! Come on out o' that flop-house! Stop shiver-
ing your guts out all day on street corners under the El.
Jesus, ain't you tired yet?

CHRISTMAS CARD

Hail Mary, Mother of God!
the new Christ child of the Revolution's about to be
born.

(Kick hard, red baby, in the bitter womb of the mob.)

Somebody, put an ad in *Vanity Fair* quick!

Call Oscar of the Waldorf—for Christ's sake!

It's almost Christmas, and that little girl—turned whore
because her belly was too hungry to stand it anymore—
wants a nice clean bed for the Immaculate Conception.

Listen, Mary, Mother of God, wrap your new born babe in
the red flag of Revolution: the Waldorf-Astoria's the
best manger we've got. For reservations: Telephone EL.
5-3000.

New Masses, December 1931

GANGSTERS

The gangsters of the world
Are riding high.
It's not the underworld
Of which I speak.
They leave that loot to smaller fry.
Why should they great Capone's
Fallen headpiece seek
When stolen crowns
Sit easier on the head—
Or Ethiopia's band of gold
For higher prices
On the market can be sold—
Or Iraq oil—
Than any vice or bootleg crown of old?
The gangsters of the world ride high—
But not small fry.

The Crisis, September 1941

4
WAR AND PEACE

Poem to a Dead Soldier

Ice-cold passion
And a bitter breath
Adorned the bed
Of Youth and Death—
Youth, the young soldier
Who went to the wars
And embraced white Death,
The vilest of whores.

Now we spread roses
Over your tomb—
We who sent you
To your doom.
Now we make soft speeches
And sob soft cries
And throw soft flowers
And utter soft lies.

We mould you in metal
And carve you in stone,
Not daring make statue
Of your dead flesh and bone,
Not daring to mention
The bitter breath
Nor the ice-cold passion
Of your love-night with Death.

We make soft speeches.
We sob soft cries.
We throw soft flowers,
And utter soft lies.
And you who were young
When you went to the wars
Have lost your youth now
With the vilest of whores.

The Workers Monthly, April 1925

To the Little Fort of San Lazaro
on the Ocean Front, Havana

Watch tower once for pirates
That sailed the sun-bright seas—
Red pirates, great romantics,

DRAKE,
DE PLAN,
EL GRILLO

Against such as these
Years and years ago
You served quite well—
When time and ships were slow.
       But now,
Against a pirate called
THE NATIONAL CITY BANK
What can you do alone?
Would it not be
Just as well you tumbled down,
Stone by helpless stone?

New Masses, May 1931

MERRY CHRISTMAS

Merry Christmas, China,
From the gun-boats in the river,
Ten-inch shells for Christmas gifts
And peace on earth forever.

Merry Christmas, India
To Gandhi in his cell,
From righteous Christian England,
Ring out, bright Christmas bell!

Ring Merry Christmas, Africa,
From Cairo to the Cape!
Ring Hallelujah! Praise the Lord!
(For murder and for rape.)

Ring Merry Christmas, Haiti!
(And drown the voodoo drums—
We'll rob you to the Christmas hymns
Until the next Christ comes.)

Ring Merry Christmas, Cuba!
(While Yankee domination
Keeps a nice fat president
In a little half-starved nation.)

And due to you down-and-outers,
("Due to economic laws")
Oh, eat, drink and be merry
With a bread-line Santa Claus—

While all the world hails Christmas,
While all the church bells sway!
While, better still, the Christian guns
Proclaim this joyous day!

While Holy steel that makes us strong
Spits forth a mighty Yuletide song:
SHOOT Merry Christmas everywhere!
Let Merry Christmas GAS the air!

New Masses, December 1930

BROADCAST ON ETHIOPIA

The little fox is still.
>The dogs of war have made their kill.

>Addis Ababa
>Across the headlines all year long.
>Ethiopia—
>Tragi-song for the news reels.
>Haile
>With his slaves, his dusky wiles,
>His second-hand planes like a child's.
>But he has no gas—so he cannot last.
>Poor little joker with no poison gas!
>Thus his people now may learn
>How Il Duce makes butter from an empty churn
>To butter the bread
>(If bread there be)
>Of civilization's misery.

MISTER CHRISTOPHER COLUMBUS

DJIBOUTI, French Somaliland, May 4 (AP) —Emperor Haile Selassie and imperial family, in flight from his crumbling empire, reached the sanctuary of French soil and a British destroyer today. . . .

HE USED RHYTHM FOR HIS COMPASS

Hunter, hunter, running, too—
Look what's after you:

PARIS, May 4 (UP)—COMMUNISTS TOP FRANCE'S
SWEEP LEFT. Minister Of Colonies Defeated. Rise From 10
To 85 Seats.

France ain't Italy!

No, but Italy's cheated
When *any* Minister anywhere's
Defeated by Communists.

Goddamn! I swear!
Hitler,
Tear your hair!
Mussolini,
Grit your teeth!
Civilization's gone to hell!
Major Bowes, ring your bell!

(GONG!)

Station XYZW broadcasting:
MISTER CHRISTOPHER COLOMBO
Just made a splendid kill.
The British Legation stands solid on its hill.
The natives run wild in the streets.
The little fox is still.

Addis Ababa
In headlines all year long.
Ethiopia—tragi-song.

American Spectator, July/August 1936

AIR RAID OVER HARLEM

Scenario for a Little Black Movie

Who you gonna put in it?
Me.
Who the hell are you?
Harlem.
Alright, then.

AIR RAID OVER HARLEM

You're not talkin' 'bout Harlem, are you?
That's where my home is,
My bed is, my woman is, my kids is!
Harlem, that's where I live!
Look at my streets
Full of black and brown and
Yellow and high-yellow
Jokers like me.
Lenox, Seventh, Edgecombe, 145th.
Listen,
Hear 'em talkin' and laughin'?
Bombs over Harlem'd kill
People like me—
Kill ME!

Sure, I know
The Ethiopian war broke out last night:
BOMBS OVER HARLEM
Cops on every corner
Most of 'em white
COPS IN HARLEM
Guns and billy-clubs
Double duty in Harlem
Walking in pairs
Under every light
Their faces
WHITE
In Harlem
And mixed in with 'em
A black cop or two
For the sake of the vote in Harlem
GUGSA A TRAITOR TOO
No, sir,
I ain't talkin' 'bout you,
Mister Policeman!
No, indeed!
I know we got to keep
ORDER OVER HARLEM
Where the black millions sleep
Shepherds over Harlem
Their armed watch keep
Lest Harlem stirs in its sleep

And maybe remembers
And remembering forgets
To be peaceful and quiet
And has sudden fits
Of raising a black fist
Out of the dark
And that black fist
Becomes a red spark

PLANES OVER HARLEM
Bombs over Harlem
You're just making up
A fake funny picture, ain't you?
Not real, not real?
Did you ever taste blood
From an iron heel
Planted in your mouth
In the slavery-time South
Where to whip a nigger's
Easy as hell—
And not even a *living* nigger
Has a tale to tell
Lest the kick of a boot
Bring more blood to his mouth
In the slavery-time South
And a long billy-club
Split his head wide
And a white hand draw
A gun from its side
And send bullets splaying
Through the streets of Harlem
Where the dead're laying
Lest you stir in your sleep
And remember something
You'd best better keep
In the dark, in the dark
Where the ugly things hide
Under the white lights
With guns by their side
In Harlem?
Say, what are yuh tryin' to do?
Start a riot?
You keep quiet!
You niggers keep quiet!

BLACK WORLD
Never wake up
Lest you knock over the cup
Of gold that the men who
Keep order guard so well
And then—well, then
There'd be hell
To pay
And bombs over Harlem

AIR RAID OVER HARLEM

Bullets through Harlem
And someday
A sleeping giant waking
To snatch bombs from the sky
And push the sun up with a loud cry
Of to hell with the cops on the corners at night
Armed to the teeth under the light
Lest Harlem see red
And suddenly sit on the edge of its bed
And shake the whole world with a new dream
As the squad cars come and the sirens scream
And a big black giant snatches bombs from the sky
And picks up a cop and lets him fly
Into the dust of the Jimcrow past
And laughs and hollers
Kiss my
!x!&!

Hey!
Scenario For A Little Black Movie,
You say?
A RED MOVIE TO MR. HEARST
Black and white workers united as one
In a city where
There'll never be
Air raids over Harlem
FOR THE WORKERS ARE FREE

What workers are free?
THE BLACK AND WHITE WORKERS—
You and me!

Looky here, everybody!
Look at me!

I'M HARLEM!

New Theatre, February 1936

Harlem, 1935

5
GOODBYE, CHRIST

To Certain "Brothers"

You sicken me with lies,
With truthful lies.
And with your pious faces,
And your wide, out-stretched
    mock-welcome, Christian hands.
While underneath
Is dirt and ugliness,
And rottening hearts,
And wild hyenas howling
In your soul's waste lands.

The Workers Monthly, July 1925

How Thin a Blanket

There is so much misery in the world,
So much poverty and pain,
So many who have no food
Nor shelter from the rain,
So many wandering friendless,
So many facing cold,
So many gnawing bitter bread
And growing old!

What can I do?
And you?
What can we do alone?
How short a way
The few spare crumbs
We have will go!
How short a reach
The hand stretched out
To those who know
No handshake anywhere.
How little help our love
When they themselves
No longer care.
How thin a blanket ours
For the withered body
Of despair!

Opportunity, December 1939

Tired

I am so tired of waiting,
Aren't you,
For the world to become good
And beautiful and kind?
Let us take a knife
And cut the world in two—
And see what worms are eating
At the rind.

New Masses, February 1931

God to Hungry Child

Hungry child,
I didn't make this world for you.
You didn't buy any stock in my railroad,
You didn't invest in my corporation.
Where are your shares in standard oil?
I made the world for the rich
And the will-be-rich
And the have-always-been-rich.
Not for you,
Hungry child.

The Workers Monthly, March 1925

A Christian Country

God slumbers in a back alley
With a gin bottle in His hand.
Come on, God, get up and fight
Like a man.

New Masses, February 1931

Goodbye, Christ

Listen, Christ,
You did alright in your day, I reckon—
But that day's gone now.
They ghosted you up a swell story, too,
Called it Bible—
But it's dead now.

The popes and the preachers've
Made too much money from it.
They've sold you to too many

Kings, generals, robbers, and killers—
Even to the Tzar and the Cossacks,
Even to Rockefeller's Church,
Even to THE SATURDAY EVENING POST.
You ain't no good no more.
They've pawned you
Till you've done wore out.

Goodbye,
Christ Jesus Lord God Jehova,
Beat it on away from here now.
Make way for a new guy with no religion at all—
A real guy named
Marx Communist Lenin Peasant Stalin Worker ME—

I said, ME—

Go ahead on now,
You're getting in the way of things, Lord.
And please take Saint Gandhi with you when you go,
And Saint Pope Pius,
And Saint Aimee McPherson,
And big black Saint Becton
Of the Consecrated Dime.
Move!

Don't be so slow about movin'!
The world is mine from now on—
And nobody's gonna sell ME
To a king, or a general,
Or a millionaire.

The Negro Worker, November/December 1932

6
THE SAILOR AND THE STEWARD/A Short Story

The Sailor and the Steward

Manuel Rojas, A. B. (not the kind of A. B. you get after four years of college, but the kind you get from chipping decks, hauling rope, washing down bulkheads and standing at the wheel) ; Able Bodied Seaman. Manuel Rojas sat in the brig and looked out through its one porthole at a blank sky, then at the blue line that was the sea's edge bobbing up and down through the round opening. Blank sky, blue sea, blank sky, blue sea—a blue-white circle cut by the horizon's line with every roll of the tramp as she steamed her way to Africa,

A hell of a place to be, in the brig, Manuel Rojas! Mid-ocean, the open sea, and you in the brig.

He ran his brown hands through his long, oily black hair, took a deep breath and rolled over on the dirty bunk. That lousy steward, maybe he couldn't get his keys out of his pocket to get to the sheets. Maybe his arm was cut clean off—and that would serve him right.

"I wish to God it was," thought Manuel Rojas.

A deep lurch to the port side and the round circle of the porthole was a solid wavy blue, the blue of sea water for just a second, then a great blank of cloudless sky again as she rolled in the opposite direction. All that Manuel had seen since the sun came up was that miniature circle of sea water and sky. And nothing to eat yet. Maybe that steward intended to let him stay in here and go hungry.

"If he does, I'll fix him when I do get ashore," Manuel announced to himself. "I'll be the last Cubano he'll ever starve."

It was getting hot as blue blazes in the little room up near the prow of that freighter rolling there off the Azores. Manuel felt mad and hungry as he pulled off his sweaty shirt and sat down in his singlet and dungarees. He felt hurt, too, and sure that someone had done him wrong. A night and a morning and he was already tired of being in the brig. He got up and paced back and forwards on the iron deck. Two steps forward, two steps backward—that's all you could pace in the brig. Finally he stopped and stuck his nose out the porthole.

"I been done wrong," he muttered to himself, turning his back on the unendingly rocking view of sea and sky. "I'll bet every sailor on this boat agrees with me—we been done wrong. We been getting the lousy end of the stick all the way out of New York this trip. And if the rest of 'em ain't men enough to fight about it, I am. Why not? What've I got to lose? Hell, this dirty tub don't mean a thing to me."

He went back and sat down on the bunk again. And right

away he realized it did mean something, too. It meant a hundred bucks to spend when he got back to Brooklyn. And a present for Azelia. And a week or ten days of ballyhoo ashore.

But maybe he'd never see Brooklyn again. Maybe that steward was dead and he, Manuel Rojas, might be tried for murder in Africa and locked up forever.

He searched his pockets for a cigarette, but he didn't have any. He got up and began to kick on the iron door and raise hell, but he knew nobody could hear him there in the brig way up in the prow by the lamp room. They had him caged, all right.

The sun beat down on the deck above his head and the little room was like a bake-oven. Damn, but he needed some water, some food, a smoke at least! He lay back down on the bunk and stared at the round rocking hole of sea and sky that was all he could sense of the world outside, that and the heat from above. He began almost to wish he hadn't cut that steward.

No, he didn't either. The dirty son of a sea-horse didn't even deserve a decent cutting. He needed to be slit, quartered, hung and dried—sending rotten food back to the crew for supper, stale bread and mushy liver stew! Who ever heard of liver stew? Only on this lousy line, in this no-good ship, had Manuel Rojas ever heard of liver stew—and he had been going to sea fourteen years, since he was twelve.

But then things were getting worse and worse on the oceans of the world. Once an able bodied seaman on a freighter got fairly good pay, but now you were lucky to get forty dollars a month, sometimes even thirty, if you got a job at all. And boats were sailing under-manned, with dumb young officers on deck and rump-sucking stewards who tried to save money "for the company."

On this ship, the *Loganderry,* what the officers had to eat one day, the crew had the leavings of the next—in hash. All the fat and gristle and bones stewed up and sent back aft to the sailors and firemen. In the saloon where the Captain, the Chief Engineer, the mates and the wireless man ate, there was fruit and meat, plenty of canned milk and sugar. But the sailors had one can of milk a day, two bowls of sugar for twenty men and never a sign of an apple or an orange. Well, most ships treated their crews pretty badly, but so far as Manuel knew none ever sent back punk liver stew before—except the *Loganderry.*

That was why he was in the brig, on account of the stew. When the apprentice boy brought back the pan smelling like nothing eatable, all the fellows at the long wooden table began to grumble. Some got up and left, and one wiper took his tin plate full and threw it out the porthole into the sea. But Manuel got up and took the container straight forward to the steward's room.

"What the hell is this?" said Manuel, and shoved it in front of his nose.

The steward shoved the pan of muddy stew right back at him and swore it was fine stuff, that the officers and everybody was eating it and that it was what the company ordered. Manuel walked into the officers' pantry and looked at the steamtable. The officers were having steaks, and a Filipino messboy in a white coat was serving them. So Manuel came back and called the steward twenty-nine names you can't put down on paper. The steward, a West Indian, bowed his head to butt, but Manuel popped him one under the chin. The steward fell clean back into his room by the desk. When he came up, he had a heavy inkwell in his hand. Then Manuel reached for a knife, switched out the blade and slashed at the steward's arm. The inkwell fell in the pan of liver stew, seasoning it an even more exotic flavor.

By that time, half the officers, including the Captain, had rushed out of the saloon, and Manuel was promptly seized, subdued and led cussing and struggling to the brig. That was last night. Now, at noon today, he was still in there, locked up.

He knew it was noon because he heard, faint and far-away, the eight bells that normally indicated the beginning of his own watch at the wheel. By now, he would have had his dinner, such as it was, and should be ready for duty.

Hell! Why didn't they bring him something to eat? Manuel turned over on his bunk and spat on the floor. His mouth was like cotton from the heat, hunger and lack of water. He was thinking of getting up and raising hell at the door again when he heard footsteps approaching on the iron deck outside.

"It's *time* somebody was coming," he growled as the door opened and in stepped the Second Mate and a Filipino messboy. The messboy had a plate of beans and a tin cup full of coffee.

"Bring me some water," Manuel commanded, sitting up on

his bunk and glowering. "This is a fine way to treat a man, trying to starve him to death."

"Didn't you have your breakfast?" the mate asked.

"No, I had no breakfast," the sailor replied, beginning to devour the beans.

"The steward must've forgot you," the mate said wryly.

"Forgot nothing!" And Manuel called the steward seventeen vile names. "He's trying to starve me to death, that's what! . . . Is he still living?"

The mate laughed. "It's a good thing you didn't do much damage with that knife of yours last night. He's all right today. Just a little scratched up. What started it, anyhow—the liver stew, heh?"

"You got it," Manuel replied. "Listen, mate, did you ever hear of liver stew?"

"Never did," said the mate who was a good fellow and had been at sea for years. "But you can't kill a man over hash."

"I can," said Manuel, as the mess boy came back with the water and departed.

"Calm down," said the mate. "The Old Man sent me back here to give you a bawling out, to tell you you're docked ten days' pay and that you're to apologize right now to the steward and come on out o' here and take your watch at the wheel."

"Apologize, hell!" said Manuel, gulping beans and water.

"Very well, then," said the mate, standing in the door, "you'll have to sit in the brig. Captain's orders, not mine. You can't buck the Old Man, you know."

"Why should I apologize to a lousy steward sending us back liver stew to eat—spoiled at that? Tell me now, why?" He put his tin plate on the floor and drank the coffee.

"How're you gonna get out then?" asked the mate.

"I'll stay in here," said Manuel. "What kind o' steward is that, trying to starve the crew? And the Captain helping him?"

"'Saving money for the company,'" said the mate, in a mocking fashion, repeating that old saying of the sea about stewards who cheat a crew's belly in order to keep up a reputation for economy.

"The company be damned!" said Manuel. "You know what it's all about, mate. Listen, you guys in the officers' mess eat pretty well, don't you? And we get what you leave a week later in hash. Fresh bread for you guys, and when it's four days old they clean out the bread box on us sailors and firemen. Always the hard ends back aft to the crew! I know the system these company-loving stewards have. But I never heard of liver stew before from nobody."

"And you're trying to break that up by cutting at the steward with a knife?"

"At least I'm trying," said Manuel.

"Well, that won't do you much good," said the mate. "The only way to stop the steward, and the company, too, from feeding you slop is for you boys back aft to get together and make one big kick in a bunch. If you don't belong to a union like we officers do, then form one. I'm talking to you like a buddy now, not like a mate."

"Yes, sir," said Manuel.

"I've been going to sea for thirty-five years, and I'm as tired as you of seeing conditions getting worse and worse, wages lower and lower, and sailors fed like dogs. But one man's flying off the handle and cutting the steward won't help any. You come on out of this brig and say 'Excuse me' to that steward, and then get your fo'c's'le mates together and organize every man back there. Savee? And next time you get liver hash, every damn one of you go up to the steward and say, 'We won't eat it.' Then you'll get something else, see? . . . You may think it's funny, me talking to you like this. But the sea's as much for the seamen who work on it as for them that owns the ships, to my way of thinking."

"You think *I* can organize a union?" Manuel asked. "Will them guys follow me?"

"Try it," said the mate. "They're all talking about you and admiring you for what you did. But they know you can't get anything for all of them, one man alone. The reason we mates don't get liver hash, too, is because we have a strong union with officers ashore. You seamen have one, but how many guys on this boat belong? Well then, get 'em together. And next time you get back in port, get your cards."

"Say," said Manuel, "you're regular! Lemme out o' this brig, mate."

Manuel's face was shining and he and the mate left the brig. A few moments later, a startled steward looked into the dancing eyes of a big beaming Cuban and thought there was certainly something phony about the apology he received. It was too glibly given.

The Anvil, July/August 1935

7
THE MEANING OF SCOTTSBORO

The Scottsboro Case, involving nine black youths indicted for allegedly raping two white prostitutes in a railroad freight car in Alabama in 1931, made headlines during the 1930s and resulted in a series of appeals and retrials before indictments against any of the defendants were dropped.

Mass support in the United States and abroad for a fair trial and freedom of the Scottsboro boys came from leading intellectuals and writers, including John Dos Passos, Theodore Dreiser, Maxim Gorki, Thomas Mann, Romain Rolland, George Bernard Shaw and H. G. Wells. Langston Hughes actively took up the cause of the Scottsboro Case through fund-raising, lecturing and writing, including his publication of Scottsboro Limited, *a collection of four poems and a play, the proceeds of which went to the Scottsboro Defense Fund. In December 1931, he visited Kilby Prison, where he read his poems to the Scottsboro inmates. The following essays express his views about the meaning of Scottsboro.*

Southern Gentlemen, White Prostitutes, Mill-Owners, and Negroes

If the 9 Scottsboro boys die, the South ought to be ashamed of itself—but the twelve million Negroes in America ought to be more ashamed than the South. Maybe it's against the law to print the transcripts of trials from a State court. I don't know. If not, every Negro paper in this country ought to immediately publish the official records of the Scottsboro cases so that both whites and blacks might see at a glance to what absurd farces an Alabama court can descend. (Or should I say an American court?) . . . The 9 boys in Kilby Prison are Americans. Twelve million Negroes are Americans, too. (And many of them far too light in color to be called Negroes, except by liars.) The judge and the jury at Scottsboro, and the governor of Alabama, are Americans. Therefore, for the sake of American justice (if there is any), and for the honor of Southern gentlemen (if there ever were any), let the South rise up in press and pulpit, home and school, Senate Chambers and Rotary Clubs, and petition the freedom of the dumb young blacks—so indiscreet as to travel unwittingly, on the same freight train with two white prostitutes . . . And, incidentally, let the mill-owners of Huntsville begin to pay their women decent wages so they won't need to be prostitutes. And let the sensible citizens of Alabama (if there are any) supply schools for the black populace of their state, (and for the half-black, too—the mulatto children of the Southern gentlemen [I reckon they're gentlemen]) so the Negroes won't be so dumb again . . . But back to the dark millions—black and half-black, brown and yellow, with a gang of white fore-parents—like me. If these twelve million Negro Americans don't raise such a howl that the doors of Kilby Prison shake until the 9 youngsters come out (and I don't mean a polite howl, either), then let Dixie justice (blind and syphilitic as it may be) take its course, and let Alabama's Southern gentlemen amuse themselves burning 9 young black boys till they're dead in the State's electric chair. And let the mill-owners of Huntsville continue to pay women workers too little for them to afford the price of a train ticket to Chattanooga . . . Dear Lord, I never knew until now that white ladies (the same color as Southern gentlemen) travelled in freight trains . . . Did you, world? . . . And who ever heard of raping a prostitute?

Contempo, December 1, 1931

Brown America in Jail.: Kilby

The steel doors closed. Locked. Here, too, was Brown America. Like monkeys in tiered cages, hundreds of Negroes barred away from life. Animals of crime. Human zoo for the cast-offs of society. Hunger, ignorance, poverty: civilization's major defects woven into a noose for the unwary. Men in jail, months and months, years and years after the steel doors have closed. Vast monotony of guards and cages. The State Penitentiary at Kilby, Alabama, in the year of our Lord, 1932.

Our Lord . . . Pilate . . . and the thieves on the cross.

For a moment the fear came: even for me, a Sunday morning visitor, the doors might never open again. WHITE guards held the keys. (The judge's chair protected like Pilate's.) And I'm only a nigger. Nigger. Niggers. Hundreds of niggers in Kilby Prison. Black, brown, yellow, near-white niggers. The guards, WHITE. Me —a visiting nigger.

Sunday morning: In the Negro wing. Tier on tier of steel cells. Cell doors are open. Within the wing, men wander about in white trousers and shirts. Sunday clothes. Day of rest. Cards, checkers, dice, story telling from cell to cell. Chapel if they will. One day of rest, in jail. Within the great closed cell of the wing, visiting, laughing, talking, *on Sunday*.

But in the death house, cells are not open. You enter by a solid steel door through which you cannot see. White guard opens the door. White guard closes the door, shuts out the world, remains inside with you.

THE DEATH HOUSE. Dark faces peering from behind bars, like animals when the keeper comes. All Negro faces, men and young men in this death house at Kilby. Among them the eight Scottsboro boys. Sh-s-s-s! Scottsboro boys? SCOTTSBORO boys. SCOTTSBORO BOYS! (Keep silent, world. The State of Alabama washes its hands.) Eight brown boys condemned to death. No proven crime! Farce of a trial. Lies. Laughter. Mob. Music. Eight poor niggers make a country holiday. (Keep silent, Germany, Russia, France, young China, Gorki, Thomas Mann, Romain Rolland, Theodore Dreiser. Pilate washes his hands. Listen Communists, don't send any more cablegrams to the Governor of Alabama. Don't send any more telegrams to the Supreme Court. What's the matter? What's all this excitement about, over eight young niggers? Let the law wash its hands in peace.)

There are only two doors in the death house. One from the world, in. The other from the world, out—to the electric chair. To DEATH. Against this door the guard leans. White guard, watching Brown America in the death house.

Silence. The dark world is silent. Speak! Dark world:

Listen, guard: Let the boys out.

Guard with the keys, let 'em out.

Guard with the law books, let them out.

Guards in the Supreme Court! Guards in the White House!

Guards of the money bags made from black hands sold in the cotton fields, sold in mines, sold on Wall Street:

Let them out!

Daily, I watch the guards washing their hands.

The world remembers for a long time a certain washing of hands. The world remembers for a long time a certain humble One born in a manger—straw, manure, and the feet of animals—standing before Power washing its hands. No proven crime. Farce of a trial. Lies. Laughter. Mob. Hundreds of years later Brown America sang: *My Lord! What a morning when the stars began to fall!*

For eight brown boys in Alabama the stars have fallen. In the death house I heard no song at all. Only a silence more ominous than song. All of Brown America locked up there. And no song.

Even as ye do unto the least of these, ye do it unto Me.

White guard.

The door that leads to DEATH.

Electric chair.

No song.

Opportunity, June 1932

8
COWARDS FROM THE
COLLEGES/An Essay

"Let no one who reads this article write me a letter demanding, 'But why didn't you bring out some of the good points?' For the express purpose and intention of this article is to bring out the bad points—some of the bad points—in many of our centers of Negro education today." *

*When the following piece was published in 1934, it was prefaced with this note from Hughes.

COWARDS FROM THE COLLEGES

Two years ago, on a lecture tour, I visited more than fifty colored schools and colleges from Morgan College in Baltimore to Prairie View in Texas. Everywhere I was received with the greatest kindness and hospitality by both students and faculties. In many ways, my nine months on tour were among the pleasantest travel months I have ever known. I made many friends, and this article is in no way meant as a disparagement of the courtesies and hospitality of these genial people—who, nevertheless, uphold many of the existing evils which I am about to mention, and whose very geniality is often a disarming cloak for some of the most amazingly old-fashioned moral and pedagogical concepts surviving on this continent.

At every school I visited I would be shown about the grounds, and taken to view the new auditorium or the modern domestic science hall or the latest litter of pigs born. If I took this tour with the principal or some of the older teachers, I would often learn how well the school was getting on in spite of the depression, and how pleasant relationships were with the white Southerners in the community. But if I went walking with a younger teacher or with students, I would usually hear reports of the institution's life and ways that were far from happy.

For years those of us who have read the Negro papers or who have had friends teaching in our schools and colleges, have been pretty well aware of the lack of personal freedom that exists on most Negro campuses. But the extent to which this lack of freedom can go never really came home to me until I saw and experienced myself some of the astounding restrictions existing at many colored educational institutions.

To set foot on dozens of Negro campuses is like going back to mid-Victorian England, or Massachusetts in the days of the witch-burning Puritans. To give examples, let us take the little things first. On some campuses grown-up college men and women are not allowed to smoke, thus you have the amusing spectacle of twenty-four-year-old men sneaking around to the back doors of dormitories like little boys to take a drag on a forbidden cigarette. At some schools, simple card playing is a wicked abomination leading to dismissal for a student—even though many students come from homes where whist and bridge are common amusements. At a number of schools, dancing on the campus for either faculty or students is absolutely forbidden. And going to dancing parties off campus is frequently frowned upon. At one school for young ladies in North Carolina, I came across an amusing rule which allowed the girls to dance with each other once or twice a week, but permitted no young men at their frolics. At some schools marching in couples is allowed instead of dancing. Why this absurd ban on ballroom dancing exists at colored schools, I could never find out—doubly absurd in this day and age when every public high school has its dances and "proms," and the very air is full of jazz, North and South, in inescapable radio waves.

One of the objects in not permitting dancing, I divined, seems to be to keep the sexes separated. And in our Negro schools the technique for achieving this—boys not walking with girls, young men not calling on young ladies, the two sexes sitting aisles apart in chapel if the institution is co-education—in this technique Negro schools rival monasteries and nunneries in their strictness. They act as though it were unnatural for a boy and girl to ever want to walk or talk together. The high points of absurdity during my tour were campuses where young men and women meeting in broad daylight in the middle of the grounds might only speak to one another, not stand still to converse lest they break a rule; and a college in Mississippi, Alcorn,—where to evening lectures grown-up students march like school kids in and out of the hall. When I had finished my lecture at Alcorn, the chairman tapped a bell and commanded, "Young ladies with escorts now pass." And those few girls fortunate enough to receive permission to come with a boy rose and made their exit. Again the bell tapped and the chairman said, "Unescorted young ladies now pass." And in their turn the female section rose and passed. Again the bell tapped. "Young men now pass." I waited to hear the bell again and the chairman saying, "Teachers may leave." But apparently most of the teachers had already left, chaperoning their grown-up charges back to the dormitories. Such regimentation as practiced in this college was long ago done away with, even in many grammar schools of the North.

Apparently the official taboo on male and female companionship extends even to married women teachers who attend summer seminars in the South, and over whom the faculty extends a prying but protective arm. The wife of a prominent educator in the South told me of being at Hampton for one of their summer sessions a few years ago. One night her husband called up long distance just to hear his wife's voice over the phone. Before she was permitted to go to the phone and talk to a MAN at night, however, she had to receive a special permit from, I believe, the dean of women, who had to be absolutely assured that it really was her husband calling. The long distance phone costs mounted steadily while the husband waited but Hampton did its part in keeping the sexes from communicating. Such interference with nature is a major aim on many of our campuses.

Accompanying this mid-Victorian attitude in manners and morals, at many Southern schools there is a great deal of official emphasis placed on heavy religious exercises, usually compulsory, with required daily chapels, weekly prayer meetings, and Sunday services. Such a stream of dull and stupid sermons, uninspired prayers, and monotonous hymns—neither intellectually worthy of adult minds nor emotionally exciting in the manner of the old time shouts—pour into students' ears that it is a wonder any young people ever go to church again once they leave college. The placid cant and outworn phrases of many of the churchmen daring to address student groups today makes me wonder why their audiences are not bored to death. I did observe many young people going to sleep.

But there are charges of a far more serious nature to bring against Negro schools than merely that of frowning on jazz in favor of hymns, or their horror of friendly communication between boys and girls on the campuses. To combine these charges very simply: Many of our institutions apparently are not trying to make men and women of their students at all—they are doing their best to produce spineless Uncle Toms, uninformed, and full of mental and moral evasions.

I was amazed to find at many Negro schools and colleges a year after the arrest and conviction of the Scottsboro boys, that a great many teachers and students knew nothing of it, or if they did the official attitude would be, "Why bring that up?" I asked at Tuskegee, only a few hours from Scottsboro, who from there had been to the trial. Not a soul had been so far as I could discover. And with demonstrations in every capital in the civilized world for the freedom of the Scottsboro boys, so far as I know not one Alabama Negro school until now has held even a protest meeting. (And in Alabama, we have the largest colored school in the world, Tuskegee, and one of our best colleges, Talladega.)

But speaking of protest meetings—this was my experience at Hampton. I lectured there the week-end that Juliette Derricotte was killed. She had been injured in an automobile wreck on her way home from Fisk University where she was dean of women, and the white Georgia hospitals would not take her in for treatment, so she died. That same week-end, a young Hampton graduate, the coach of Alabama's A.&M. Institute at Normal was beaten to death by a mob in Birmingham on his way to see his own team play. Many of the Hampton students and teachers knew Juliette Derricotte, and almost all of them knew the young coach, their recent graduate. The two happenings sent a wave of sorrow and of anger over the campus where I was a visitor. Two double tragedies of color on one day—and most affecting to students and teachers because the victims were "of their own class," one a distinguished and widely-travelled young woman, the other a popular college graduate and athlete.

A note came to me from a group of Senior students asking would I meet with a student committee. When a young man came to take me to the meeting, he told me that it would concern Juliette Derricotte and their own dead alumnus. He said that the students wanted to plan a protest on the campus against the white brutality that had brought about their death.

I was deeply touched that they had called me in to help them, and we began to lay plans for the organization of a Sunday evening protest meeting, from which we would send wires to the press and formulate a memorial to these most recent victims of race hate. They asked me would I speak at this meeting and I agreed. Students were chosen to approach the faculty for permission to use the chapel. We were to consult again for final plans in the evening.

At the evening committee meeting the faculty had sent their representative, Major Brown, a Negro (who is, I believe, the dean of men), to confer with the students. Major Brown began by saying that perhaps the reports we had received of the manner of these two deaths had not been true. Had we verified those reports?

I suggested wiring or telephoning immediately to Fisk and to Birmingham for verification. The Major did not think that wise. He felt it was better to write. Furthermore, he went on, Hampton did not like the word "protest." That was not Hampton's way. He, and Hampton, believed in moving slowly and quietly, and with dignity.

On and on he talked. When he had finished, the students knew quite clearly that they could not go ahead with their protest meeting. (The faculty had put up its wall.) They knew they would face expulsion and loss of credits if they did so. The result was that the Hampton students held no meeting of protest over the mob-death of their own alumnus, nor the death on the road (in a Negro ambulance vainly trying to reach a black hospital) of one of the race's finest young women. The brave and manly spirit of that little group of Hampton students who wanted to organize the protest was crushed by the official voice of Hampton speaking through its Negro Major Brown.

More recently, I see in our papers where Fisk University, that great (?) center of Negro education and of Jubilee fame has expelled Ishmael Flory, a graduate student from California on a special honor scholarship, because he dared organize a protest against the University singers appearing in a Nashville Jim-crow theatre where colored people must go up a back alley to sit in the gallery. Probably also the University resented his organizing, through the Denmark Vesey Forum, a silent protest parade denouncing the lynching of Cordie Cheek who was abducted almost at the very gates of the University.

Another recent news item tells how President Gandy of Virginia State College for Negroes called out the cracker police of the town to keep his own students from voicing their protest as to campus conditions. Rather than listen to just grievances, a Negro president of a large college sends for prejudiced white policemen to break his students' heads, if necessary.

And last year, we had the amazing report from Tuskegee of the school hospital turning over to the police one of the wounded Negroes shot at Camp Hill by white lynchers because the share-croppers have the temerity to wish to form a union—and the whites wish no Negro unions in Alabama.

Without protest, the greatest Negro school in the world gives up a poor black, bullet-riddled share-cropper to white officers. And awhile later Tuskegee's president, Dr. Moton, announces himself in favor of lower wages for Negroes under the N.R.A., and Claude Barnett, one of his trustees, voices his approval of the proposed code differentials on the basis of color.

But then, I remember that it is Tuskegee that maintains a guest house on its campus for *whites only!* It also maintains a library that censors all books on race problems and economics to see that no volumes "too radical" get to the students. And during my stay there several young teachers whispered to me that a local white trustee of the school receives his Negro visitors only on the porch, not in his house. It is thus that our wealthiest Negro school with its two thousand six hundred students expects to turn out men and women!

Where then would one educate "Uncle Toms?"

Freedom of expression for teachers in most Negro schools, even on such unimportant matters as to rouge or not to rouge, smoke or not smoke, is more or less unknown. Old and moss-backed presidents, orthodox ministers or missionary principals, control all too often what may or may not be taught in the classrooms or said in campus conversation. Varied examples of suppression at the campuses I visited are too numerous to mention in full in a short article, but they range all the way from an Alabama secondary school that permitted no Negro weeklies like the *Chicago Defender* or the *Pittsburgh Courier* in its library because they were "radical," to the great university of Fisk at Nashville where I asked a nationally known Negro professor and author of several books in his field what his attitude toward communism was, and received as an answer, "When I discuss communism on this campus, I will have a letter first from the president and the board of trustees."

There is at the Negro schools in the South, even the very well-endowed and famous ones that I have mentioned, an amazing acquiescence to the wishes of the local whites and to the traditions of the Southern color-line. When programs are given, many schools set aside whole sections in their own auditoriums for the exclusive use of whites. Often the best seats are given them, to the exclusion of Negro visitors. (But to insert into this article a good note, Mary McLeod Bethune, however, permits no such goings-on at Bethune-Cookman Institute in Daytona, one of the few campuses where I lectured that had not made "special provisions" for local white folks. A great many whites were in the audience but they sat among the Negroes.)

Even where there is no official campus segregation (such as Tuskegee's white guest house, or Hampton's hospital where local whites are given separate service) , both teachers and students of Negro colleges accept so sweetly the customary Jim Crowing of the South that one feels sure the race's emancipation will never come through its intellectuals. In North Carolina, I was given a letter to the state superintendent of the Negro schools, a white man, Mr. N. C. Newbold. When I went to his office in Raleigh to present my letter, I encountered in his outer office a white woman secretary busy near the window quite a distance from the door. She gave me a casual glance and went on with what she was doing. Then some white people came into the office. Immediately she dropped her work near the window and came over to them, spoke to them most pleasantly, and ignored me entirely. The white people, after several minutes of how-are-you's and did-you-enjoy-yo'self-at-the-outing-last-week, said that they wished to see Mr. Newbold. Whereupon, having arrived first and having not yet been noticed by the secretary, I turned and walked out.

When I told some Negro teachers of the incident, they said, "But Mr. Newbold's not like that."

"Why, then," I asked, "does he have that kind of secretary?"

Nobody seemed to know. And why had none of the Negro teachers who call at his office ever done anything about such discourteous secretaries? No one knew that either.

But why (to come nearer home) did a large number of the students at my own Lincoln University, when I made a campus survey there in 1929, declare that they were opposed to having teachers of their own race on the faculty? And why did they then (and probably still do) allow themselves to be segregated in the little moving picture theatre in the nearby village of Oxford, when there is no Jim-Crow law in Pennsylvania—and they are some four hundred strong? And why did a whole Lincoln University basketball team and their coach walk docilely out of a cafe in Philadelphia that refused to serve them because of color? One of the players explained later, "The coach didn't want to make a fuss."

Yet Lincoln's motto is to turn out leaders! But can there be leaders who don't want to make a fuss?

And can it be that our Negro educational institutions are

not really interested in turning out leaders at all? Can it be that they are far more interested in their endowments and their income and their salaries than in their students?

And can it be that these endowments, incomes, gifts—and therefore salaries—springing from missionary and philanthropic sources and from big Northern boards and foundations—have such strings tied to them that those accepting them can do little else (if they wish to live easy) but bow down to the white powers that control this philanthropy and continue, to the best of their ability, to turn out "Uncle Toms?"

A famous Lincoln alumnus, having read my undergraduate survey of certain deplorable conditions on our campus, said to me when I graduated there, "Your facts are fine! Fine! Fine! But listen, son, you mustn't say everything you think to white folks."

"But this is the truth," I said.

"I know, but suppose," continued the old grad patronizingly, in his best fatherly manner, "suppose I had always told the truth to white folks? Could I have built up that great center for the race that I now head in my city? Where would I have gotten the money for it, son?"

The great center of which he spoke is a Jim Crow center, but he was very proud of having built it.

To me it seems that the day must come when we will not be proud of our Jim Crow centers built on the money docile and lying beggars have kidded white people into contributing. The day must come when we will not say that a college is a great college because it has a few beautiful buildings, and a half dozen Ph.D.'s on a faculty that is afraid to open its mouth though a lynching occurs at the college gates, or the wages of Negro workers in the community go down to zero!

Frankly, I see no hope for a new spirit today in the majority of the Negro schools of the South unless the students themselves put it there. Although there exists on all campuses, a distinct cleavage between the younger and older members of the faculties, almost everywhere the younger teachers, knowing well the existing evils, are as yet too afraid of their jobs to speak out, or to dare attempt to reform campus conditions. They content themselves by writing home to mama and by whispering to sympathetic visitors from a distance how they hate teaching under such conditions.

Meanwhile, more power to those brave and progressive students who strike against mid-Victorian morals and the suppression of free thought and action! More power to the Ishmael Florys, and the Denmark Vesey Forum, and the Howard undergraduates who picket the Senate's Jim Crow dining rooms—for unless we develop more and ever more such young men and women on our campuses as an antidote to the docile dignity of the meek professors and well-paid presidents who now run our institutions, American Negroes in the future had best look to the unlettered for their leaders, and expect only cowards from the colleges.

The Crisis, August 1934

9
PORTRAIT AGAINST BACKGROUND

In June 1932, Langston Hughes traveled to Russia with twenty-two Afro-Americans at the invitation of the Meschrabpom Film Corporation to make a motion picture entitled BLACK AND WHITE. *The film was never made, for reasons explained by Hughes himself in the piece "Moscow and Me".*

He remained in the Soviet Union for one year. The following selections reflect the impact of the USSR upon him.

Moscow and Me

"If you can't carry from New York, then buy in Berlin. Everything: Canned goods, sugar, soap, toilet paper, pencils, ink, winter clothes, can openers, toothbrushes, shoestrings, and so on, and so on, and so on. Otherwise you will go hungry, dirty and ragged in Moscow," thus good friends earnestly advised me.

"You will be guided, guarded and watched all the time in Moscow—the G.P.U.," they warned me.

"The peasants and poor folks have control and they're the stupidest people on earth. You will be sadly disappointed in Moscow," estimable gentlemen who had especially studied the "Russian experiment" told me.

"Oh, and what might happen to your poetry! There's only propaganda in Moscow," charming ladies with artistic souls exclaimed.

"They only want to make Communists out of you-all, you and the rest of these Negroes going in that group—and get you slaughtered when you come back home—if the American government lets you come back," genteel colored people told me. "You'd better stay home."

"Can't," I said. "I want to see Moscow."

So when the *Europa* sailed from New York on June 14 in the year of our one-time Lord 1932, there I was in a group of 22 Negroes going to the Soviet Union to make a film, *Black and White!*

Moscow met us at Leningrad—in the persons of some of the officials of the Meschrabpom for whom we were to work. And among them was a Negro! None of these men from Moscow appeared pale and undernourished or in need of the canned goods we had brought. And certainly colored Comrade Whiteman didn't look anything like

> *A motherless chile*
> *A long ways from home.*

And he has lived in Moscow for years.

The banquet they spread for us at the October Hotel in Leningrad ran all the way from soup on through roast chicken and vegetables right down to ice cream and black coffee. And an orchestra playing dinner music. All of which was

> *Better, better, that I gets at home.*

The speeches were short and warm with proletarian greetings and the orchestra played the *Internationale:*

> *Arise, ye prisoners of starvation.*

But we were all a little too full of good food at the moment to give that line its real meaning.

> *Arise, ye slaves no more in thrall.*

We did better on that; we Negroes: Moscow and freedom! The Soviet Union! The dream of all the poor and oppressed—like us—come true.

> *You have been naught,*
> *You shall be all.*

We slept on the Express roaring through the night toward Moscow. In the morning we emerged from the train to the clicking of a battery of newspaper cameras and the greetings of a group of Moscovites come to meet us. And among them were two more Negroes! One was Emma Harris who's lived in Russia for thirty years, sings, and makes the best apple pies in the world. And the other was a grandly black boy whom we thought was from Africa—but who turned out to be from Chicago. His name was Bob.

Our hands were shaken. We were hugged and kissed. We were carried along in the crowd to the bright sunshine of the street outside. And there a flock of long shiny cars waited for us—Buicks and Lincolns—that swept us through the Moscow boulevards making as much time as the taxis in Central Park. We drove across the Red Square past Lenin's Mausoleum and the towers and domes of the Kremlin—and stopped a block away at the Grand Hotel.

Our rooms were ready for us—clean and comfortable, with hot and cold water, homelike settees and deep roomy chairs. Courteous attendants there were, baths and elevator, a book shop and two restaurants. Everything that a hotel for white folks at home would have—except that, quite truthfully, there was no toilet paper. And no Jim Crow.

Of course, we knew that one of the basic principles of the Soviet Union is the end of all racial distinctions. That's the main reason we had come to Moscow.

That afternoon another long table was spread in the hotel dining room, and we ate again. Around this welcoming board we met our first Russian friends. And learned to say, "Tovarish." And thus began our life in Moscow, the Red Capital.

Here there should follow several pages about how we made the movie that we had come to take part in—except that the movie was not made! Why? Well, here's the inside dope. A few days after I got here I was contracted to revise the dialogue so, with an interpreter, I sat in at most of the conferences. I listened to Pudovkin, Eck, and other famous cinema experts analyze and dissect the proposed script for *Black and White* as prepared for filming. There were heated discussions on every scene and every line of dialogue. There were a dozen different disagreements. The defects of the plot and continuity were mercilessly exposed. And finally the production of a picture based on the scenario at hand was called off.

Moving picture studios all over the world are, after all, more or less alike. Pictures are listed and cancelled. Directors are hired and fired. Films are made and shelved. What happened to *Black and White* in Moscow, happens to many films in Hollywood. But between the studios of Hollywood and those of Moscow there is this difference: In Hollywood the production of films is quite frankly a business for the making of money. In Moscow the production of films is quite frankly an art for the advancement of certain ideas of social betterment. In Hollywood, too, writers, directors, and producers will squabble over a scenario for weeks, but in the end, if the artistic ideals of the writers are opposed to the money-making ideals of the producers, the artistic ideals go and box-office appeal takes their place. In Moscow, on the other hand, the profit-making motif is entirely absent. It has no need for being, as the films do not necessarily depend on the box office for their funds. And the endless arguments that go on between scenario writers, directors, and producers center rather around how to present with the greatest artistic force the ideals that will make for the betterment of the Soviet people. In Moscow, the aim is to create a socially important film. In Hollywood, it is to make money.

So when the best minds of the Soviet film industry declared the scenario of *Black and White* artistically weak and unsound; and when they said that they felt it could not do justice to the oppressed and segregated Negroes of the world, or serve to further enlighten Soviet movie audiences, there could hardly have been a better reason for the postponement of the film until a more effective scenario could be prepared. Nevertheless, a few of the members of our group, loath to leave the comforts of the Grand Hotel and return to Harlem, shouted loudly that the black race of the whole world had been betrayed, and they themselves had been cheated and disillusioned. Even after they had been paid in full for the four months of our contract, fare in dollars reimbursed, and sent home via Paris, some few still continued to weep in the Harlem papers about the evils of Moscow which housed a film company that would not make a bad picture from a weak scenario—so they could act in it. One can understand that attitude, however, so great is the urge to go in the movies, even among us Negroes. Many an aspirant has left Hollywood cursing Metro-Goldwyn-Mayer. But between leaving Hollywood and Moscow there is this difference: Many disappointed would-be screen stars depart from Hollywood hungry. Our Negro artists left Moscow well-fed, well paid, and well entertained, having been given free excursions that included Odessa, the Black Sea, Central Asia, Tiflis, and Dneprostroi. They went home via London, Paris, or Berlin. Or they could have stayed (and several did) with offers of parts in other films or jobs in Moscow. But I hear from New York that a few are still mad because they could not immediately star in *Black and White,* be the scenario good or bad.

O, Movies. Temperaments. Artists. Ambitions. Scenarios. Directors, producers, advisors, actors, censors, changes, revisions, conferences. It's a complicated art—the cinema. I'm glad I write poems.

After three months of the movies, I was delighted to pack my bags and go off on a plain prose-writing assignment to Central Asia for a study of the new life there around Bukhara and Samarkand—socialism tearing down the customs of ages: veiled women, concubinage, mosques, Allah-worship, and illiteracy disappearing. When I came back to Moscow in the winter, those of our Negro group who had remained, seven in all, had settled down comfortably to life in the Soviet capital. Dorothy West was writing, Mildred Jones taking screen tests for a new picture. Long, tall Patterson who paints houses had married a girl who paints pictures, and together they have executed some of the finest decorations for the May Day celebration. Wayland Rudd was studying singing, fencing and dancing, and taking a role in a new Meyerhold play. McKenzie stayed in the films, working for Meschrabpom. And Homer Smith, as a special consultant in the Central Post Office, was supervising the installation of an American special delivery system for Moscow mail. So the Negroes made themselves at home. Some were getting fat.

After five months in Asia, I was glad to be back in Moscow again—great, bustling city comparable in some ways to Chicago, Cleveland or New York. But very different, too. For instance, in the American cities money is the powerful and respected thing. In Moscow, work is powerful—and not money. One can have ever so many rubles and still find many places and pleasures closed to him. Food, lodging, theatre tickets, medical service, all the things that dollars buy at home, are easily available in Moscow only if one is a worker and has the proper papers from one's factory, shop, office or trade union. I was glad I belonged to the International Union of Revolutionary Writers. Credentials were far more important than rubles.

And another thing that makes Moscow different from Chicago or Cleveland, or New York, is that in the cities at home Negroes—like me—must stay away from a great many places—hotels, clubs, parks, theatres, factories, offices, and union halls —because they are not white. And in Moscow, all the doors are open to us just the same of course, and I find myself forgetting that the Russians are white folks. They're too damn decent and polite. To walk into a big hotel without the doorman yelling at me (at my age), "Hey, boy, where're you going?" Or to sit at the table in any public restaurant and not be told, "We don't serve Negroes here." Or to have the right of seeking a job at any factory or in any office where I am qualified to work and never be turned down on account of color or a WHITE ONLY sign at the door. To dance with a white woman in the dining room of a fine restaurant and not be dragged out by the neck—is to wonder if you're really living in a city full of white folks (as is like Moscow).

But then the papers of the other lands are always calling the Muscovites red. I guess it's the red that makes the difference. I'll be glad when Chicago gets that way, and Birmingham.

For me, as a writer, Moscow is certainly different, too. It's the first city I've ever lived in where I could make my living entirely from writing. Not that I write more here than I do elsewhere, but I am paid better, and there is a wider market. In America the magazines in which one can frequently publish stories or poems about Negroes are very few, and most of these do not pay, since they are of a social service or proletarian nature. The big American bourgeois publications are very careful about what they publish by or about colored people. Exotic or humorous tales they will occasionally use. Stories that show Negroes as savages, fools, or clowns, they will often print. And once in a blue moon there may be a really sound and serious literary picture of black life in a big magazine—but it doesn't happen often enough to feed an author.

They can't live on blue moons. Most colored writers find their work turned down with a note that the files are already full of "Negro material," or that the subject is not suitable, or, as happened to me recently when I submitted a story about a more or less common situation in American interracial life—the manuscript was returned with regrets since the story was "excellently written, but it would shock our good middle-class audience to death." And thus our American publications shy away from the Negro problem and the work of Negro writers.

In Moscow, on the other hand, the editors welcome frank stories of American Negro life. They print them and pay for them. Book publishers welcome volumes by black writers, and, in spite of the paper shortage, a great many books of Negro life have appeared in translation in Moscow. Large audiences come to hear colored writers lecture on their work, and dinners and testimonials are given in their honor. There is no segregated Harlem of literature in Moscow.

As to writers in general, I feel safe in saying that members of the literary craft, on the whole, live better in the Soviet Union than they do in America. In the first place there is a tremendous reading public buying millions of books, papers, and magazines, in dozens of different languages. Translation rights of a Soviet writer's work here within the Union alone may bring in thousands of rubles. And there are, in Moscow and other cities, cooperative dining rooms for writers, specially built modern apartments with very low rents, excellent clubs and tennis courts and libraries—all for the workers in words.

As for me, I received for one edition of my poems in translation more money in actual living value than I have yet made from the several editions of my various volumes of poetry in America. For an edition in Uzbek, a minority language that most Americans never heard of (nor I either till I came here), I was paid enough to live in grand style for a year or modestly for two years—which is more than poetry alone ever did for me at home.

There is in Moscow a great curiosity for things American, and a great sympathy for things Negro. So, being both an American and a Negro, I am met everywhere with friendly questions from children and adults as to how we live at home. Is there really a crisis, with people hungry and ragged when there are in America so many factories, so much technique, so much wheat, and cotton and livestock? How can that be? Do they actually kill people in electric chairs? Actually lynch Negroes? Why?

The children in the Moscow streets, wise little city children, will ofttimes gather around you if you are waiting for a streetcar, or looking into a shop window. They will take your hand and ask you about the Scottsboro boys, or if you like the Soviet Union and are going to stay forever. Sometimes as you pass a group of children playing, they will stop and exclaim, "Negro!" But in wonder and surprise a long ways from the insulting derision of the word "Nigger" in the mouths of America's white children. Here, the youth in the schools are taught to respect all races. And at the Children's Theatre there is a sympathetic play being given of how a little Negro girl found her way from Africa to Moscow, and lived happily ever after.

Strangers in general meet with widespread courtesy from the citizens of Moscow. *Inastranyetz,* they will say, and let you go to the head of the line, if there is a crowd waiting at the stamp window in the post office, or standing in the queue for an auto bus, or buying tickets to the theatre. If you go alone to the movies, someone is sure to offer to translate for you, should they happen to know a little German or English. If you hand a written address to a citizen on a Moscow street, often said citizen will go out of his way to lead you to the place you are seeking. I have never lived in a more truly courteous city. True, there is not here anywhere in public places the swift and efficient directness of America. Neither is there the servile, tip-chasing, bowing and scraping service of Paris. But here there is friendliness. In Moscow there are often mountains and swamps of red tape that would drive you crazy, were it not for the gentle patience and kindnesses of the ordinary citizens and simple workers anxious to offer to strangers their comradely help and extend their services as hosts of the city. So in spite of the entirely new routine of life which Moscow offers, it does not take one long to feel at home.

Of course, there is the room problem, for the city is the most over-crowded in the world. A foreigner coming to Moscow (unless as a tourist) should really bring a room with him. The great Eisenstein, maker of marvellous movies, lives in only one room. In spite of hundreds of new apartments that have been built, the growth of housing has not been able to keep up with the growth of the populace. A Moscow apartment is as crowded as a Harlem flat at the height of the great Negro migration from the South. Yet, with all their own housing difficulties, the Muscovite can listen patiently to irate foreign workers who are indignant at not immediately receiving on arrival a three-room apartment with kitchenette and bath.

The Negroes whom I know in Moscow are all housed comfortably and are not as much given to complaints as certain other nationalities who come to the workers' capital with a greater superiority complex as to their world importance. The colored people in Moscow move easily in Russian circles, are well received, and cordially welcomed in private homes, in workers' clubs, and at demonstrations. There are always dark faces in the tremendous May Day demonstrations that move for hours through the Red Square. A great many Negroes took part in the gigantic Scottsboro Demonstration in the summer of 1932 at the Park of Rest and Culture. The pictures of Negro workers are often displayed in the windows of shops on the main Moscow streets. During the recent May holidays there was a huge picture of Robinson, the colored *udarnik* at the Ball Bearing Plant, on display in a busy part of Gorky Street. Moscow's black residents are well woven into the life of this big proletarian city, and they are received as comrades.

As for me, I've had a swell time. I've spoken at demonstrations, read poems at workers' clubs, met lots of poets and writers and artists and actors, attended all the leading theatres from the Opera to Ohlopkov's Realistic Theatre where the stage is all round the audience and you sit in the middle. I've seen the finest Gauguins and Cézannes in the world, have eaten soup with the Red Army, danced with the Gypsies, and lived excitingly well, and have done a great deal of writing.

I shall go back to America just as clean (there is soap here), just as fat (and food), just as safe and sound (and the G.P.U.) as I was when I left New York. And once there I'm thinking that I'll probably be homesick for Moscow. There's an old Negro song that says:

You never miss the water till the well runs dry. Those who ought to know, tell me that you never really appreciate Moscow until you get back again to the land of the bread lines, unemployment, Jim Crow cars and crooked politicians, brutal bankers and overbearing police, three per cent beer and the Sottsboro Case.

Well, the Russian workers and peasants were awfully patient with the Tsar, but when they got rid of him—they really *got rid* of him. Now they have a right to be proud of their red flags flying over the Kremlin. They put them there. And don't let anybody in America kid you into believing what with talking about lack of soap and toilet paper and food and the G.P.U., that Moscow isn't the greatest city in the world today. Athens used to be. Then Rome. And more recently, Paris. Now they'll put you in jail in Alabama for even mentioning Moscow! That's one way of recognizing its leadership.

Moscow, 1933

International Literature, July 1933

GOING SOUTH IN RUSSIA

To an American Negro living in the northern part of the United States the word *South* has an unpleasant sound, an overtone of horror and of fear. For it is in the South that our ancestors were slaves for three hundred years, bought and sold like cattle. It is in the South today that we suffer the worst forms of racial persecution and economic exploitation—segregation, peonage, and lynching. It is in the Southern states that the color line is hard and fast, Jim Crow rules, and I am treated like a dog. Yet it is in the South that two-thirds of my people live: a great Black Belt stretching from Virginia to Texas. across the cotton plantations of Georgia and Alabama and Mississippi, down into the orange groves of Florida and the sugar cane lands of Louisiana. It is in the South that black hands create the wealth that supports the great cities—Atlanta, Memphis, New Orleans, where the rich whites live in fine houses on magnolia-shaded streets and the Negroes live in slums restricted by law. It is in the South that what the Americans call the "race problem" rears its ugly head the highest and, like a snake with its eyes on a bird, holds the whole land in its power. It is in the South that hate and terror walk the streets and roads by day, sometimes quiet, sometimes violent, and sleep in the beds with the citizens at night.

Two springs ago I came almost directly out of this American South to the Soviet Union. You can imagine the contrast. No need for me to write about it. And after a summer in Moscow, I found myself packing up to go South again—but, this time, South under the red flag. I was starting out from Moscow, capital of the new world, bound for Central Asia to discover how the yellow and brown peoples live and work there. I wanted to compare their existence with that of the colored and oppressed peoples I had known under capitalism in Cuba, Haiti, Mexico, and my own United States. I wanted to study the life of these dark people in the Soviet Union, and write a book about them for the dark races of the capitalist world.

On the train I had a lot of time to think. I thought how in the thirty years of my life I had seldom gotten on a train in America without being conscious of my color. In the South, there are Jim Crow cars and Negroes must ride separate from the whites, usually in a filthy antiquated coach next to the engine, getting all the smoke and bumps and dirt. In the South, we cannot buy sleeping car tickets. Such comforts are only for white folks. And in the North where segregated travel is not the law, colored people have, nevertheless, many difficulties. In auto buses they must take the seats in the rear, over the wheels. On the boats they must occupy the worst cabins. The ticket agents always say that all other accommodations are sold. On trains, if one sits down by a white person, the white person will sometimes get up, flinging back an insult at the Negro who has dared to take a seat beside him. Thus it is that in America, if you are yellow, brown, or black, you can never travel anywhere without being reminded of your color, and oft-times suffering great inconveniences.

I sat in the comfortable sleeping car on my first day out of Moscow and remembered many things about trips I had taken in America. I remembered how, once as a youngster going alone to see my father who was working in Mexico, I went into the dining car of the train to eat. I sat down at a table with a white man. The man looked at me and said, "You're a nigger, ain't you?" and left the table. It was beneath his dignity to eat with a Negro child. At St. Louis I went onto the station platform to buy a glass of milk. The clerk behind the counter said, "We don't serve niggers," and refused to sell me anything. As I grew older I learned to expect this often when traveling. So when I went South to lecture on my poetry at Negro universities, I carried my own food because I knew I could not go into the dining cars. Once from Washington to New Orleans, I lived all the way on the train on cold food. I remembered this miserable trip as I sat eating a hot dinner on the diner of the Moscow-Tashkent express.

Traveling South from New York, at Washington, the capital of our country, the official Jim Crow begins. There the conductor comes through the train and, if you are a Negro, touches you on the shoulder and says, "The last coach forward is the car for colored people." Then you must move your baggage and yourself up near the engine, because when the train crosses the Potomac River into Virginia, and the dome of the Capitol disappears, it is illegal any longer for white people and colored people to ride together. (Or to eat together, or sleep together, or in some places even to work together.) Now I am riding South from Moscow and am not Jim-Crowed, and none of the darker people on the train with me are Jim-Crowed, so I make a happy mental note in the back of my mind to write home to the Negro papers: "There is no Jim Crow on the trains of the Soviet Union."

In the car ahead of mine there is a man almost as brown as I am. A young man dressed quite ordinarily in a pair of tan trousers and a nondescript grey coat. Some Asiatic factory worker who has been to Moscow on a vacation, I think. We talk a little. He asks me what I do for a living, and I ask him what he does. I am a writer. He is the mayor of Bokhara, the Chairman of the City Soviet! I make a note in the back of my mind: "In the Soviet Union dark men are also the mayors of cities," for here is a man who is the head of a very famous city, old Bokhara, romantic Bokhara known in stories and legends the world over.

In the course of our conversation, I learned that there were many cities in Central Asia where dark men and women are in control of the government. And I thought about Mississippi where more than half of the population is Negro, but one never hears of a colored person in the government. In fact, in that state Negroes cannot even vote. And you will never meet them riding in the sleeping car.

Here, there were twelve of us going South from Moscow, for I was traveling with a Negro group from Meschrabpom Film on a tour of the Soviet Union.

Kurbanov, for that was the name of the young Uzbek from the Bokhara Soviet, came often to talk to us. He was a mine of information about the liberation of Central Asia and the vast changes that have come about there after the Revolution. Truly a land of Before and After. Before the Revolution, emirs and khans, mullahs and beys. After the Revolution, the workers in power. Before, one-half of one per cent of the people illiterate. Now, fifty percent read and write. Before, education solely for the rich, mostly in religious schools; and no schools in the villages. Now, free schools everywhere. Before, the land was robbed of its raw materials for the factories of the Russian capitalists. Now, there are big plants, electric stations, and textile mills in Asia. Before, no theatres, no movies, no modern culture. Now, national art encouraged and developed everywhere. Before, Kurbanov said, the natives were treated like dogs. Now, that is finished, and Russian and native, Jew and gentile, white and brown, live and work together. Before, no intermarriages of white and brown, now there are many. Before, Kurbanov himself was a herd-boy in the mountains. Now, he is the Chairman of a city Soviet, the mayor of a large and ancient city. Truly, Soviet Asia is a land of Before and After, and the Revolution is creating a new life that is changing the history of the East.

We gathered these things not only from our Uzbek comrade, but from many other passengers we met on the long train during the five days and nights southeast to Central Asia. There was a woman librarian from Leningrad, who had been home on a vacation going back to the work of which she spoke with pride—the growth of the library at Tashkent, the large number of books in the native languages with the new Latin alphabet that were now being published, and the corresponding growth of native readers. There was a young Red Army man who told us of the camaraderie and understanding growing up between lads of widely different environmental backgrounds in the Red Army School at Tashkent. There was a Russian merchant privileged to help in the building of new industries in an ancient and once backward, but now awakening Asia. And there were two young Komsomol poets going from Moscow to work on publications for the encouragement of national literature in the young writers of Soviet Asia.

One night, we held a meeting with the members of the train crew not then on duty. Our Negro group and the workers of the express exchanged information and ideas. They told us about their work and their part in the building of socialism. We told them about the conditions of Negro labor in America, about the crisis abroad, about Al Capone and the Chicago bandits, and the bootleggers and bankers of Broadway. We found that they knew, as their comments and questions indicated, a great deal more about America than the average American knows about the Soviet Union. And we learned that their working conditions are superior to those of American railway workers—particularly in regard to the train porters. Here, in each coach, there is a compartment with berths where the crew might rest. The Negro porters on American trains have no such conveniences. Here, on the sleeping cars, there are two attendants. In the U.S.A. a single man takes care of a car, working throughout a long trip, and perhaps managing to catch a little sleep on the bench in the men's toilet. Our porters depend on tips for a living, their wages being extremely low. These things we told the crew of the Moscow-Tashkent express and they, in turn, sent back through us their greetings to the Negro railway workers of America.

So, with our many new and interesting comrades of the train, the days on the road passed quickly. First, the rich farm lands slid by outside our windows; stations where peasant women from the *kolkhozes* sold chickens and cheese and eggs; then the Volga at sunset, famous old river of song and story; a day or so later. Orenburg where Asia begins and camels are in the streets; then the vast reaches of the Kirghiz steppes and the bright tip of the Aral Sea like silver in the sun.

On the day when we passed through the Kazakhstan desert, the Fortieth Anniversary of Gorki's literary life was being celebrated throughout the Union. The Komsomol poets and the crew of our train organized a meeting, too. At a little station where the train stopped in the late afternoon, we all went on to the platform and short speeches were made in honor of Gorki and his tremendous work. (Even in the heart of the desert, this writer whose words throbs with the lives of the common people, was not forgotten.) Nomad Kazakhs, the men in great coats of skins, the women in white headdresses, gathered around, mingling with the passengers. One of the young poets spoke; then a representative of the train crew; and someone from the station. My speech in English was translated into Russian, and again into the Kazakh tongue. Then the meeting closed. We sent a telegram to Comrade Gorki from the passengers of the train, and another from our Negro group. And as the whistle blew, we climbed back into our coaches, and the engine steamed on through the desert pulling the long train deeper into Asia. It was sunset, and there was a great vastness of sky over sand before the first stars came.

Late the following afternoon, we saw a fertile oasis of water and greenery, cotton growing and trees in fruit, then crowds of yellow faces and bright robes at the now frequent stations. At evening we came to the big city of Tashkent, the great center of the Soviet East. There we were met by a workers' delegation including brown Asiatics, fair-skinned Russians, and an American Negro engineer, Bernard Powers, from Howard University, helping to build roads across Asia.

The Crisis, June 1934

THE SOVIET UNION

There is ONE country in the world that has NO JIM CROW of any sort, NO UNEMPLOYMENT of any sort, NO PROSTITUTION or demeaning of the human personality through poverty, NO LACK OF EDUCATIONAL FACILITIES for all of its young people, and NO LACK OF SICK CARE or dental care for everybody. That country is the Soviet Union.

In 1947 the Soviet Union will be 30 years old as a political entity. Emerging from the feudalism of the Russian Tzarist Empire with its serfdom, ignorance, and Asiatic slavery, in a quarter of a century the peoples of the Soviet Union have achieved these world-shaking social improvements—which puts it well ahead of every other country in the world insofar as human decency stemming from government goes.

I have been in the Soviet Union, so I am not speaking from theory or long distance information read in books. I have never been a member of the Communist party so I am not speaking (as some may be inclined to accuse) from political bias. I do not claim that the Soviet Union is a paradise. It is not. But the steps toward an earthly paradise reach higher today on the soil of the Soviet Union than they do anywhere else in this troubled world. And the future of the Soviet Union is based on more concrete modern social achievements than that of any other existing state.

I am tremendously impressed by the fact that this country, comprising one-sixth of the earth's surface and almost two hundred different nationalities of varying colors, has NO Jim Crow, NO anti-semitism, and NO racial prejudice. That alone is enough to attract toward the Soviet the sympathies of colored peoples the world over.

As a poor man myself working many hours a day all my life for a meagre living, I am tremendously impressed by a country that has no unemployment, where people need not be afraid of starvation because there may not be (often as here in our America) any work for them to do. Remembering well, as I do, the days of our great depression with members of my own family on home relief, WPA, and in CCC camps, with the streets of the Negro sections of Los Angeles, Chicago, and New York shadowed by women selling their bodies for the price of a cheap meal, I am tremendously impressed by a country where body and soul destroying depressions no longer take place, and where what food resources they have are more or less equally distributed.

During my lifetime, I have seen relatives and friends go for months without proper medical attention simply because they did not have the money to pay for it. I have seen persons wearing ill-fitted glasses because there was no cash for new ones, and others suffering aching teeth because they had no funds for emergency dental care. So I was deeply impressed in the Soviet Union to see suffering people receive medical attention immediately WITHOUT CHARGE.

When I saw these things in the Soviet Union, they seemed almost like miracles to me. I had never seen anything like that in Jim Crow Kansas where I grew up, or in Cleveland or Harlem where I later lived, or in Boston or Birmingham or San Antonio or Hollywood where I travelled. And no place in America had I ever been absolutely sure that I, a Negro, could go into any restaurant or public place and buy a meal. But there was never any doubt of such service in the Soviet Union.

That is perhaps why I was so amazed and shocked the other day to hear at the annual assembly of the American Academy of Arts and Letters in New York, where I was awarded a grant, a Senator from Arkansas, the Hon. J. William Fulbright, jump on the Soviet Union with both feet, stating in his address against Russia that ". . . we are willing and able to fight whenever we believe any power threatens the right and opportunity of men to live as free individuals under a government of their own choice." (As if such freedom existed in Arkansas.)

Senator Fulbright's attack on the one country in the world that has equality for all races, seemed to me to come with ill grace from a white lawmaker from one of our most illiterate and color-prejudiced states in poll-tax Dixie where the basic right of the ballot is still largely denied colored citizens. But I have seen all around the world from Africa to China, the gall of white Nordics who segregate in Nigeria, set up Jim Crow YMCAS in Shanghai, and draw the color line on India. So I should not have been amazed at our Senator from Arkansas. Perhaps he is so willing to fight the Soviet Union because he knows that once Soviet ideas spread over the world, people will get tired of poor schools, Jim Crow—and Senator Fulbright.

The Chicago Defender, June 1, 1946

The Soviet Union and Jews

Years ago when I was a child in Kansas, summer evenings on the front porch or winter evenings by the stove in the kitchen, my grandmother used to read to me from the daily paper or from the Negro weeklies that we took, usually the *Topeka Plain-Dealer* or *The Chicago Defender.*

Very early in life, it seemed to me that there was a relationship between the problems of the Negro people in America and the Jewish people in Russia, and that the Jewish people's problems were worse than ours. In my child mind, I think the relationship came about in this way. Ever so often my grandmother would read a headline in the Negro press stating that a Negro had been lynched in Georgia, or two Negroes had been lynched in Louisiana, or three Negroes had been lynched in Texas.

From our daily paper ever so often she would read an item that a dozen Jews had been ridden down by the horses of the Cossacks in the Ukraine, or 50 Jews killed in a pogrom in Old Russia, or a hundred Jews killed and injured by a mob in Poland. So, I thought, here in our American South we Negroes were lynched by one or twos or threes, but in Tzarist Russia and Poland they killed Jews by the dozens, or even the hundreds.

As I grew older, and went to high school in Cleveland, and mingled with Jewish students of Russian parentage, I learned that in Old Russia there were many schools to which Jews could not go—just as we have schools in America to which Negroes may not go. I learned that there were even towns and cities where Jews could not live—just as we have towns where Negroes cannot live. I learned that the police of Old Russia and Poland gave Jewish people very little protection from mob violence—just as American police give but little protection to the Negro people.

While I was in high school the Russian Revolution took place and the Soviets took power. Among the Jewish students in my American high school there was much jubilation because, they said, the Soviets did not believe in anti-Semitism, and that there were Jews high in the government now. In 1932 when I went to Russia, I was curious to see what real changes had taken place in the status of the Jewish people since Tzarist days. I knew that the Jewish problem in Old Russia must have been as deep-seated as is the Negro problem in my own country.

In the new Soviet Union I found no Jewish problem. I found no towns or cities from which Jews were still barred. I found no schools that refused to admit them. I found no more pogroms against Jews, and no one who dared openly insult or spit on Jews as was done in the old days. In less than fifteen years, I found that Soviet Russia had gotten rid of the Jewish problem.

Jews attended schools and taught in the schools just as other Soviet citizens might do. Jews voted and were elected to office equally with other citizens. Many leading Soviet officials were Jews. Many high in the arts and professions were Jews. Gone were the days of insults and pogroms because one was not a Nordic and a gentile. Gone—in less than fifteen years—was the Jewish problem!

In Moscow I asked how these things were achieved. I was told that the whole theory of the Communist state was opposed to the separation of peoples on religious or racial grounds, and that workers had no strength divided up into warring camps. I was told the Soviet schools taught that all men are equal.

I said, "The theory of our American democracy is that all men are equal, too—except that where I live it does not seem to work out that way. Theories are all right—but how do you make them work in Russia?"

"Here we have laws against racial intolerance," they said.

I said, "We have such laws in some of our American cities, too, but often the laws do not work."

The Russians said, "In the Soviet Union, we make them work. Here nobody dares insult or spit on or hurt a Jew simply because he is a Jew any more. If anyone does that, he's put in jail. After he stays in jail awhile, he does not come out and soon insult or harm a Jew again, not very likely. But if a person persists in his racial prejudice, then he is put in jail for a long time. So people have stopped insulting Jews here—that is, the people who still might wish to do so. But no Communist, no real Soviet citizen would think of doing so anyway, nor would any child educated in our schools. Such a thing would be uncomradely—not to speak of being bad manners."

So I learned that the Soviet government had not only made laws and enforced them against racial intolerance, but had also taught people good manners, which seemed to me a wonderful thing to be doing. In Washington, D. C., in this year of our Lord, 1946, not even the grand ladies of the D.A.R. know how to behave politely.

The Chicago Defender, June 8, 1946

The Soviet Union and Color

A quarter of a century ago just after World War I, speaking of his visit to the Soviet Union, the great American journalist, Lincoln Steffens, said, "I have seen the future—and it works!"

In 1943 in his book, *One World,* the late Wendell Willkie wrote of his trip throughout the Soviet Republics, "Russia is an effective society. It works."

One of the things that impressed me most deeply when I was in the Soviet Union is that their laws against race prejudice really work. Before the Soviet Revolution in 1917 the Jews were treated much as Hitler treated them in Nazi Germany, and the colored subjects of the Tzar were Jim Crowed as I am Jim Crowed in America. Today all of that stupid racism is gone in the Soviet Republics. In less than thirty years anti-Semitism and color prejudice have all disappeared over one-sixth of the earth's surface.

The Russians and the Ukrainians are white, but there are many colored peoples in the Soviet Union. The Yakuts in the North are colored, and the Uzbeks, the Turkomens, the Tajiks in the South are colored. By our American standards even the Tartars might be Jim Crowed south of Washington, D.C. And certainly the Mongols would be treated in California as badly as Americans treat Japanese or Filipinos or Negroes. In old Russia and its colonies, the Tzars treated these peoples badly, too.

When I was in Tashkent, the regional capital of the Republics of Soviet Central Asia, there were funny little old street cars running about the size of the cable cars in San Francisco. I noticed a partition at the center of these streetcars, and asked a brownskin Uzbek friend why it was there. He explained to me that in the old Tzarist days, that partition separated the Europeans from the Asiatics.

I said, "You mean the white people from the colored people?"

He said, "Yes, before the Revolution, we would have to sit in the back. But now everybody sits anywhere."

I thought to myself how many white Americans say it will take a hundred years, or two or three generations, to wipe out segregation in the South. But in Tashkent it had taken only a few years—and a willingness on the part of the government to enforce decent racial laws.

In a museum in Ashkabad, capital of Turkmenia, I saw signs on the wall as curiosities for the school kids to look at: SARTS KEEP OUT, in both the Turkomen and Russian language. I was told that in the old days these signs were at the entrances of the big beautiful public park in the heart of Ashkabad. In Tzarist times that park was only for Europeans— white people, not for the native peoples whom the whites contemptuously termed "sarts," a word equivalent to our worst anti-Negro terms.

As I stood looking at these signs in a museum now, but once very real barriers to the colored peoples of Turkmenia, I remembered parks I had seen in my own America where I could not enter—public parks in cities like Charleston and Memphis and Dallas. Even today after a great world war for democracy, such parks still exist in our United States. They are gone in the Soviet Union.

As in India today, or South Africa, there were formerly humiliating and difficult travel restrictions and educational and political limitations applied by the Tzarist Russians against their Asiatic colonies.

The Soviet government has wiped out all of these restrictions. People who less than thirty years ago had to travel under Jim Crow conditions, now travel as freely as anyone else. People who could not vote because of their race or colonial status, now vote as freely as others, and elect members of their own group to all of the Soviet lawmaking bodies. Whole groups of people whom the Tzars never permitted to have schools, now have schools—even colleges and medical schools.

In his *One World*, Willkie reported that the Yakuts were formerly only two per cent literate—just a few could read and write. But by 1940 education had made such progress that the figures were reversed—now there are only two per cent that cannot read and write.

So from Jim Crow cars to freedom, from helplessness to the ballot, from ignorance to schools, from scorn—"sarts"—to decency and respect as Soviet citizens, from being nobodies, serfs and semi-slaves to having a part in their own government—that is how far the colored peoples of the Soviet Union have come in a little over twenty-five years. So there is a clear example in the world to prove to our American "experts" in race relations that it DOES NOT TAKE A HUNDRED YEARS, it does NOT take generations to get rid of ugly, evil, antiquated, stupid Jim Crow practices—if a country really wants to get rid of them.

The Chicago Defender, June 15, 1946

THE SOVIET UNION AND WOMEN

Even more impressive than the changes for the better in race relations in the Soviet Union, is the vast improvement in the position of women there. In both the Asiatic and European portions of the Union since the revolution, the level of women has been lifted greatly.

Work for all, state educational funds for the young, and old-age pensions for the aged have wiped out prostitution completely. There is no longer any need for any woman to sell her body through hunger, or the desire to go to college, or to care for herself when age is creeping on. In many great cities of the capitalist world, I have seen poor girls of high school age selling their favors as cheaply as a pair of stockings. And I have seen women too old to be appealing to men still trying to earn a few dollars with their bodies. During the American depression, the streets of our big cities were full of such women. Poverty, the economic root of prostitution, is gone in the Soviet Union.

In the Tzarist days in Russia, only women of the top middle and upper classes received an education. It was almost unheard of for poor working girls to have a chance to go to school. Educational opportunities for poor people were far more limited in Imperial Russia than they are even in Mississippi today. And when a family could afford to send one child to school, it was the boy who got the chance, not the girl. Now all that is changed, and girls are educated equally with boys in the Soviet Republics. Jews and colored Asiatics, formerly hindered by quotas or no-admittance policies in Tzarist schools are no longer so restricted, which means that women and men of minority groups have the same educational advantages as other Soviet citizens.

The change in the position of women in the republics of Soviet Asia is even more striking than in European Russia. In Uzbekistan and Turkmenistan before 1924—when the British armies withdrew and permitted Soviet ideals to penetrate those former Tzarist colonies—women were virtual slaves. Men kept harems and women were bought and sold. The daughters of poor families were purchased by rich men for their harems. A poor man had a hard time getting a wife at all since only the ugliest, oldest, and least desirable women were left for his poor price.

Once in a harem, women could leave—even do a little shopping—only when the lord and master permitted. Then they were always guarded by older women and servants. Harem life was very dull, so I was told by former harem inmates in Tashkent and Samarkand. Having no education, the women could not read. Most of the time they simply sat around the courtyard combing each other's hair, or quarreling. And that courtyard, by the way, was a sort of backyard corral—the front of the house and its fine gardens being largely reserved for the men of the family.

Uzbek women were formerly among the most heavily veiled in the Orient. The thin little half-veils of Turkey and Arabia were not for them. In Uzbekistan, before the Soviets came to power, all grown women had to wear the "paranja," a heavy black horse-hair veil from head to foot, through which their faces could not be seen, and through which they themselves could scarcely see. In Uzbekistan today some of the older women still wear this veil through custom or fear of their husbands, but Soviet law permits them to cast it aside if they wish, and no young women wear veils any more. One of the oldest customs of the Orient has thus been broken by the new Soviet freedoms for women in Central Asia.

As in the old Chinese and Japanese theatres, only men appeared as actors and dancers in Tzarist Asia before the revolution. Art and culture were not for women. Custom did not permit them to appear in public except heavily veiled. A woman was only for her husband's harem pleasure. But today the stage and concert halls are open to women throughout the

Sovietized parts of Asia. Tamara Khanum, whom I met and interviewed, was the first unveiled female Uzbek dancer to dance on the stage in the late 1920s. This was such an innovation in cities like Bokhara and Samarkand that the state had to supply a company of soldiers to guard her to keep the reactionary men-folks from tearing her from the stage. But today hundreds of women take part in Uzbek plays and concerts, so soldiers are no longer necessary.

Most of the women of Soviet Central Asia now have thrown away their veils, are no longer bought and sold, are free of harems, and are being educated in Soviet schools in ideals of freedom for all. From a land of Jim Crow, exploitation, and harems, Soviet Central Asia has become the most advanced portion of the Orient and an equal part of the entire great Soviet Union.

The Chicago Defender, June 29, 1946

THE SOVIET UNION AND HEALTH

When I was in the Soviet Union, with Arthur Koestler, then a Berlin newspaper reporter (now better known as the author of *Darkness At Noon* and other famous novels), I paid a visit to a collective farm in a remote corner of the Republic of Uzbekistan. The farm was way down in the heart of Asia near the Afghanistan border, not far from where the northernmost tip of India almost touches Soviet territory.

Over the Soviet borders there was a steady trickle of immigrants from Afghanistan and India, mostly poor peasants from Beluchistan. These immigrants had heard that in the Soviet Union no beys or emirs or princes or colonial overlords robbed the poor of the fruits of their labor. They had heard that there the irrigation ditches were not controlled by the rich, and that no man had to till another man's fields in order to have the use of a little water for his own. The collective farm that Koestler and I visited was peopled entirely by turbaned Beluchi tribesmen.

The men and women there were as brown as I am—in other words, a definitely colored people. The only white person on that farm—in fact, the only European for miles around—was a young and quite beautiful Russian nurse. She was in charge of the clinic and all of the health work for these Indian peasant farmers. She delivered their babies, nursed their sick, cured malaria, and fought inherited venereal disease. She taught them that modern science and hygiene are better than old customs and superstitions—such as putting an axe under the bed to hasten child-birth, or washing new born babies in sand.

I was deeply impressed with efforts such as this which the Soviet Government was making everywhere I went to care for the health of even the most backward of its peoples. But I was even more impressed later when, having a toothache myself, I received treatment without charge, simply by showing my card as a guest-member of the Soviet Writers' Union. I learned that all workers in the Soviet Union were entitled to such health service. And I could not help remembering how in my America one often went without treatment for lack of money.

All over the Soviet Union medical schools were open to all without regard to race or color. There is no quota system for Jews or non-white peoples such as we still have here in the United States. In Samarkand and other Asiatic cities, great medical centers were being built for people who under the Tzars and Emirs, had not even had grade schools, let alone medical schools.

Hospitals were not closed to patients on account of race. A few years before I went to Russia, a great Negro woman YWCA worker, Juliette Derricotte, known and respected by Negro youth all across America, had died in the South because, after an automobile accident, no hospital along the road where she was injured would admit her since she was not white.

A few months ago, since our war for democracy was fought, I was the guest of a Negro physician during my southern lecture tour. His charming and cultured wife had recently been taken suddenly ill, requiring emergency attention. But the only hospital bed that could be secured for her in that town was in the damp and mouldy basement of the local hospital— for it was in the basement that ALL Negro patients were placed, with only a screen between the men and the women. And no Negro physician could practice in that hospital. Negro doctors could not attend their own patients there. Prejudiced white nurses slapped and abused colored patients at will.

Nothing like that goes on in the Soviet Union. The color line in health, as in all other walks of life, has disappeared there. In the hospital at Tashkent, I saw Europeans and Asiatics together in the same wards. And there were both Russians and Uzbek physicians in attendance.

There is still a very great need for skilled doctors and surgeons in our United States. But this very summer of 1946, the New York papers have carried news of investigations of several of our great medical schools that either bar entirely or have very small quotas for Americans of Jewish, Negro, or Italian descent. There is a great need in America for nurses, but many nursing schools will not admit colored girls. Jim Crow is like a dagger in the back of America's health program.

We are a great and rich country. There is no good reason why anybody should have to live with the toothache for lack of money. There is no reason why anybody should be denied treatment or hospitalization because of race. There is no good reason why an American Jew or Italian or Japanese or Negro should be limited to only a handful of hospitals at which such minority citizens may intern after finishing medical school—if they are ever lucky enough to get into medical school under our segregated quota systems. From the Soviet Union our country can learn much concerning the morals of medicine.

The Chicago Defender, July 20, 1946

FAULTS OF THE SOVIET UNION

The Soviet Union is not a perfect country. It is not a paradise on earth. It is by no means peopled by angels. Its peoples are human beings just as we are. They make mistakes. They do wrong. They have not created as yet a heaven here on this terrestrial globe. But they are not as bad as some of the books published in this country and many of our newspapers have made them out to be. The American standard of living, even for poor people, is higher than that of most other countries of the world. Years ago when I travelled about the world as a seaman, I learned that little things like a radio, or a kodak, or a wristwatch were luxuries in many lands, whereas in our own country even the poorest person can manage to get hold of one or the other without trying too hard. And a Ford car—well you just about have to be rich to own a car of any sort in Europe or Asia. That, of course, is why immigrants have flocked to America from all over the world.

Americans are notoriously bad travellers and complain

loudly about the inconveniences they encounter abroad. They get mad when they cannot find orange juice in Europe or Coca-Colas in Asia. And nowhere else on earth do you find that marvellous institution, the American drug store, with everything from an aspirin to apple pie, an alarm clock to a dictionary.

I do not believe there was an orange in the whole Soviet Union when I was there, nor even orange juice in a can. Certainly there was no apple pie, and I do not believe you could buy an alarm clock anywhere. One could not purchase a pencil, either, that would write more than 20 words without wearing down to the wood, or breaking off. Coca-Colas were unheard of. Little physical lacks such as these irritated many American visitors very much, and I think even turned some completely anti-Soviet.

Great big bulky newspapers with news from all over the world, sports, a condensed novel, comics, and lots of pictures every day, are missing, too. And Soviet radio programs, when I was there, were as monotonous as their restaurant menus. Just as they lacked a wide variety of foods, so they lacked the Lone Ranger, Backstage Wife, Bing Crosby, and the Ford Hour, not to mention commercials. Soviet street cars and trains were as crowded as ours during war-time. And theatre tickets anywhere were as hard to secure as they are for hit shows on Broadway. Houses and apartments were hard to get, too. In fact, almost everything was scarce—but what there was was made to go around more or less equally to everyone.

Freedom of speech in the American sense was lacking in the Soviet Union. You could not get up in public and make a speech denouncing the heads of the government, nor could you publicly denounce Jews and Negroes, as Bilbo, Rankin, and Talmadge do in our country. For doing such over there you would be put in jail and locked up good. Soviet newspapers do not go in for crime news, nor for items derogatory to any racial group. Nice juicy murders and big black brutes are both missing from their pages. Soviet headlines are not as exciting in a sensational way as ours.

The Soviet Union is far from being a communist country in a theoretical or practical sense. At the moment socialism is what they have achieved. Salaries and living conditions are still unequal. But nobody can profit from or exploit the labor of another. What one makes must be made from one's own labor, initiative, and intelligence. And nobody much can make a million dollars—just as very few in our own country can make a million—although millions here still suffer that illusion. But in the Soviet Union nobody need fear poverty, either, since all basic human needs, food, health care, jobs, child care, education, are planned for by the state to benefit ALL THE PEOPLE.

I have written mostly about the things I liked about the Soviets, because they far overbalance the things I don't like, and because I think our America can learn some good things about race relations, democratic education and health programs, and insurance against poverty from the Soviet people. I would also like to see our country and their country be friends, not enemies.

Naturally, I have been asked the question, "Well, if you like Russia so much, why don't you go there and stay?" Here is my answer: I don't go there and stay because this is my home, the U.S.A. I was born in the very middle of it. It is mine—faults and all—and I had rather stay here and help my country get rid of its faults—race prejudice, economics inequalities, and Bilbo—than to run away.

The Chicago Defender, August 3, 1946

LIGHT AND THE SOVIET UNION

One of my most vivid memories from my year in the Soviet Union is the memory of a visit to Chirchikstroy—meaning the Chirchik River Dam—one chilly evening. Chirchikstroy is in the deep heart of Soviet Central Asia not far from the borders of India and China—way down in the storied region of Samarkand and Bokhara.

As a foreign writer visiting in a nearby city, I was the especially invited guest to what might seem to many a very humble celebration in a remote rural region. The celebration was the opening of the first workers' barracks at the site where the new dam, Chirchikstroy, was to be constructed. Since it was a damp chilly day, and since I have never cared too much about the country even under ideal weather conditions, I was almost on the verge of declining the invitation to go and look at nothing more than a workers' barracks. Had the dam been built, perhaps I might want to see that—but a barracks, well, I was doubtful.

I am eternally glad that I went, however, because in my short visit to the banks of the Chirchik River, I found the whole human meaning of the Soviet Union and its material and spiritual significance to the world of tomorrow. An uneducated young worker there put into five short words the entire meaning of the Union of Socialist Soviet Republics—and his five short words took in the whole world, not just his own people or his own land.

In the late afternoon, about the time when, had it not been drizzling rain, the more faithful of the Moslems could have been seen bowing down in the dust toward Mecca, we left the big Oriental city in a rickety car headed for Chirchikstroy. As we drove over the country roads past mud huts and country Chai-hanas (tea houses) decorated with red bunting and pictures of Soviet heroes, I thought about the Uzbek past of autocratic beys and emirs, Tzarist military overlords, serfs, harems, veiled women, human beings bought and sold, dirt, poverty, and disease.

In Ashkabad, Merv, Samarkand, I had seen new schools, hospitals, youth clubs where Soviet teachers and officials were fighting against the old ugly heritage of the past. I had seen young people impatient that the standards of a thousand years were not changing fast enough, impatient that not all women had discarded their ancient horsehair veils and thrown off the shackles of the harems, that not all men had given up their ideas of tyranny and the feudal age. In Soviet Central Asia I had seen a land and a people in transition more marked even than that of European Russia. At the end of my rickety auto ride I was to hear in five short symbolic words the meaning of all that projected around the world and forward into time beyond our day.

The fellow who wrapped it all up into five words was an unprepossessing looking little guy of unknown ancestry, maybe Tartar, maybe Tajik. He was short and stocky and homely. His skin was a kind of dirty yellow and his short wiry hair was the same color. American Negroes would call him "meriney." He looked like he might be 16 or 17 years old. He was a member of the Reception Committee that greeted me at the door of a long wooden hut on a barren stretch of ground as our car drove up in the pitch black of a country night. A country village and a few mud huts, vague shapes of machinery—steam shovels, perhaps—I had seen nearby in the darkness, but I could not see in the dark the river whose waters were to be dammed.

The eternal tea of the Orient was going around piping hot

in its little bowls. There was a festive air, and though not a word of any of their language could I understand, my translator got over to me much of the conversation and the meaning of the folk songs that came later in the evening. But it was the little "meriney" guy who sort of took me in tow and who showed me every corner of the cleanly scrubbed barracks and the wooden bunks—all built, he said, by the men themselves in their spare time after work as their gift to the building of this new dam—the first modern dam in that part of Asia. And it was in speaking of the dam that the little guy said the five words that wrapped it all up.

He said, "Then there will be light." He told me how there were only candles and lanterns and tallow flares now, and most of the villagers in the mud huts scarcely had those. "But," he said, "when the dam is built, there will be light! And not just for us," he said, "but for all the world, too, because this dam will be so powerful that we can send light over the borders into India and into China! That is why we do not mind giving our labor after hours to build this first building here—this workers' barracks—and we will give many extra hours to that dam, too—because when it is done—tell your people in your America—when it is done, there will be light! Light to study by and to see—and it won't be dark any more!"

The Chicago Defender, August 10, 1946

Lenin

Lenin walks around the world.
Frontiers cannot bar him.
Neither barracks nor barricades impede.
Nor does barbed wire scar him.

Lenin walks around the world.
Black, brown, and white receive him.
Language is no barrier.
The strangest tongues believe him.

Lenin walks around the world.
The sun sets like a scar.
Between the darkness and the dawn
There rises a red star.

New Masses, January 22, 1946

10
DARKNESS IN SPAIN

In 1937, Hughes spent six months in Spain covering events of the Spanish Civil War as a correspondent for The Afro-American Newspapers. *During that time he also wrote numerous poems about the war, in an expression of his strong support for the Loyalist cause. Some of those works appear on the following pages.*

Before he entrained for the Spanish front (a trip during which he encountered visa difficulties) he delivered a speech in Paris to the International Writers' Congress, the text of which follows here.

The speech made by Langston Hughes, delegate from the United States, to the Second International Writers Congress, Paris, July, 1937.

Too Much of Race

Members of the Second International Writers Congress, comrades, and people of Paris: I come from a land whose democracy from the very beginning has been tainted with race prejudice born of slavery, and whose richness has been poured through the narrow channels of greed into the hands of the few. I come to the Second International Writers Congress representing my country, America, but most especially the Negro peoples of America, and the poor peoples of America—because I am both a Negro and poor. And that combination of color and of poverty gives me the right then to speak for the most oppressed group in America, that group that has known so little of American democracy, the fifteen million Negroes who dwell within our borders.

We are the people who have long known in actual practice the meaning of the word Fascism—for the American attitude towards us has always been one of economic and social discrimination: in many states of our country Negroes are not permitted to vote or to hold political office. In some sections freedom of movement is greatly hindered, especially if we happen to be sharecroppers on the cotton farms of the South. All over America we know what it is to be refused admittance to schools and colleges, to theatres and concert halls, to hotels and restaurants. We know Jim Crow cars, race riots, lynchings, we know the sorrows of the nine Scottsboro boys, innocent young Negroes imprisoned some six years now for a crime that even the trial judge declared them not guilty of having committed, and for which some of them have not yet come to trial. Yes, we Negroes in America do not have to be told what Fascism is in action. We know. Its theories of Nordic supremacy and economic suppression have long been realities to us.

And now we view it on a world scale: Hitler in Germany with the abolition of labor unions, his tyranny over the Jews, and the sterilization of the Negro children of Cologne; Mussolini in Italy with his banning of Negroes on the theatrical stages, and his expedition of slaughter in Ethiopia; the Military Party in Japan with their little maps of how they'll conquer the whole world and their savage treatment of Koreans and Chinese; Batista and Vincent, the little American-made tyrants of Cuba and Haiti; and now Spain and Franco with his absurd cry of "Viva España" at the hands of Italians, Moors and Germans invited to help him achieve "Spanish Unity." Absurd, but true.

We Negroes of America are tired of a world divided superficially on the basis of blood and color, but in reality on the basis of poverty and power—the rich over the poor, no matter what their color. We Negroes of America are tired of a world in which it is possible for any group of people to say to another: "You have no right to happiness, or freedom, or the joy of life." We are tired of a world where forever we work for someone else and the profits are not ours. We are tired of a world where, when we raise our voices against oppression, we are immediately jailed, intimidated, beaten, sometimes lynched. Nicolás Guillén has been in prison in Cuba, Jacques Roumain, in Haiti, Angelo Herndon in the United States. Today a letter comes from the great Indian writer, Raj Anand, saying that he cannot be with us here in Paris because the British police in England have taken his passport from him. I say, we darker peoples of the earth are tired of a world in which things like that can happen.

And we see in the tragedy of Spain how far the world oppressors will go to retain their power. To them now the murder of women and children is nothing. Those who have already practiced bombing the little villages of Ethiopia now bomb Guernica and Madrid. The same Fascists who forced Italian peasants to fight in Africa now force African Moors to fight in Europe. They do not care about color when they can use you for profits or for war. Japan attempts to force the Chinese of Manchuria to work and fight under Japanese supervision for the glory and wealth of the Tokyo bourgeoisie—one colored people dominating another at the point of guns. Race means nothing when it can be turned to Fascist use. And yet race means everything when the Fascists of the world use it as a bugaboo and a terror to keep the working masses from getting together. Just as in America they tell the whites that Negroes are dangerous brutes and rapists, so in Germany they lie about the Jews, and in Italy they cast their verbal spit upon the Ethiopians. And the old myths of race are kept alive to hurt and impede the rising power of the working class. But in America, where race prejudice is so strong, already we have learned what the lies of race mean—continued oppression and poverty and fear—and now Negroes and white sharecroppers in the cotton fields of the South are beginning to get together; and Negro and white workers in the great industrial cities of the North under John L. Lewis and the c.i.o. have begun to create a great labor force that refuses to recognize the color line. Negro and white stevedores on the docks of the West coast of America have formed one of the most powerful labor unions in America. Formerly the unorganized Negro dockworkers—unorganized because the white workers themselves with their backward ideology didn't permit Negroes in their unions—formerly these Negro workers could break a strike. And they did. But now both Negroes and whites are strong. We are learning.

Why is it that the British police seized Raj Anand's passport? Why is it that the State Department in Washington has not yet granted me permission to go to Spain as a representative of the Negro Press? Why is it that the young Negro leader, Angelo Herndon, was finding it most difficult to secure a passport when I last saw him recently in New York? Why? We know why!

It is because the reactionary and Fascist forces of the world know that writers like Anand and myself, leaders like Herndon, and poets like Guillén and Roumain represent the great longing that is in the hearts of the darker peoples of the world to reach out their hands in friendship and brotherhood to all the white races of the earth. The Fascists know that we long to be rid of hatred and terror and oppression, to be rid of conquering and of being conquered, to be rid of all the ugliness of poverty and imperialism that eat away the heart of life today. We represent the end of race. And the Fascists know that when there is no more race, there will be no more capitalism, and no more war, and no more money for the munition makers, because the workers of the world will have triumphed.

The Volunteer for Liberty, August 23, 1937

The Crisis, September 1937

FRANCO AND THE MOORS

MADRID

Down through the Catalonian countryside our car went speeding, through villages as old as the Romans, and out along the Mediterranean, bright and blue as the morning sky. Straight across the Mediterranean—Italy. To the North,

France. And here, Spain. The Latin lands. Italy, Fascist, France, democratic. Spain torn between Fascism and democracy.

Why had I come to Spain? To write for the colored press. I knew that Spain once belonged to the Moors, a colored people ranging from light dark to dark white. Now the Moors have come again to Spain with the Fascist armies as cannon fodder for Franco. But, on the Loyalist side there are many colored people of various nationalities in the International Brigades. I want to write about both Moors and colored people.

I sat comfortably in the back seat of the car beside that excellent colored writer, Nicolás Guillén, who had come from Cuba, representing *Mediodia*, of which he is the editor. We were headed South to Valencia on the way from Barcelona, the night after an air raid, driving through fields of wheat and groves of olives and oranges, and cities that recently had been bombed from the air or shelled from the sea. And as the tragic and beautiful landscape went by. I began to think back over the first stages of my trip to Spain.

As our car sped southward toward Valencia that sunny morning, I could see quite plainly for myself that the Spanish people didn't want to be enslaved to anyone, native or foreign.

As we passed, peasants in the fields lifted their clenched fists in the government salute. On walls ruined by Fascists' bombardments, slogans were freshly painted hailing the People's Army. In the villages, young men were drilling to go to the front.

The beautiful landscapes of Spain rolled by as our car went down the road, the Spain that now for more than a year occupied the headlines on the front pages of the world. The Spain of the huge meetings I had attended at home, with three and four thousand-dollar collections given for food and medical supplies, and milk for babies.

The new democratic Spain that I had seen placarded in the main streets of cities like Denver and Salt Lake City when I lectured there. AID REPUBLICAN SPAIN! MILK FOR THE BABIES OF SPANISH DEMOCRARY! The Spain for which Josephine Baker in Paris had danced at a benefit for child refugees and for which Paul Robeson had sung in London.

A colored band, too, from the Paris Moulin Rouge had played in honor of the Second International Writers' Congress just returned to France from Madrid, having in attendance the French African writer, René Maran, the French West Indian poet, Léon Damas, and the Haitian poet, Jacques Roumain, as well as Nicolás Guillén and myself—five colored writers, each from a different part of the world.

Within the last year, colored people from many different countries have sent men, money, and sympathy to Spain in her fight against the forces that have raped Ethiopia, and that clearly hold no good for any poor and defenseless people anywhere. Not only artists and writers with well-known names, the Paul Robesons and René Marans of international fame, but ordinary colored people like those I met in the Cuban club in Barcelona, and like Carter, the ambulance driver, or the nurse from Harlem! These especially are the people I want to write about in Spain.

Naturally I am interested in the Moors, too, and what I can find out about them. As usually happens with colored troops in the service of white imperialists, the Moors have been put in the front lines of the Franco offensives in Spain—and shot down like flies. They have been brought by the thousands from Spanish Morocco where the Fascists took over power in the early days of their uprising.

First, the regular Moorish cavalry and guard units came to Spain; then civilian conscripts forced into the army, or deceived by false promises of loot and high pay. When they got to Spain, as reputable newspaper correspondents have already written, they were often paid off in worthless German marks which they were told would be good to spend when they got back to Africa.

But most of the Moors never live to get back to Africa. Now, in the second year of the war, they are no longer a potent force in Franco's army. Too many of them have been killed!

What I sought to find out in Spain was what effect, if any, this bringing of dark troops to Europe had had on the Spanish people in regard to their racial feelings. Had prejudice and hatred been created in a land that did not know it before? What has been the treatment of Moorish prisoners by the Loyalists? Are they segregated and ill-treated? Are there any Moors on the government's side?

As I thought of these things, our car began to slow down and I noticed that the traffic had grown heavier on the road. Burros, trucks, and ox-carts mingled in long lines of dust. Fords and oxen, the old and the new! Peasants on mule-back, soldiers in enormous American-made trucks. On either side of us there were orange groves as far as one could see. And in the distance, tall medieval towers mingled with modern structures. We were approaching a city, a big city.

"Valencia," the chauffeur said.

Valencia, ancient Mediterranean seaport, and now the seat of the Spanish government. I had been there twelve years ago as a sailor in the days when there was a king on the throne in Spain. Now, the people themselves are in power and democracy prevails—except that the rich, the generals, and the former friends of the king are trying to smash this democracy and have hired Franco to put the country back in chains again.

To help them do this, they called in professional soldiers, Italians, Germans, and Moors, to crush the duly elected government. Only four regiments of the regular army remained with the government, so the government had to form its own army, the People's Army, made up of farmers and working men.

To help this People's Army, and to fight Fascism before it makes any further gains in the world, men came to Spain from all over the earth. They formed the International Brigades. In these brigades there are many colored people. To learn about them, I came to Spain.

The Afro-American Newspapers, October 30, 1937

The preceding piece originally appeared in slightly different form as the second in a series of three articles written by Hughes from Spain for *The Afro-American Newspapers*. It was condensed for this volume, and the title supplied by the editor.

NEGROES IN SPAIN

MADRID

In July, on the boat with me coming from New York, there was a Negro from the far West on his way to Spain as a member of the 9th Ambulance Corps of the American Medical Bureau. He was one of a dozen in his unit of American doctors, nurses, and ambulance drivers offering their services to Spanish democracy.

When I reached Barcelona a few weeks later, in time for my first air raid and the sound of bombs falling on a big city, one of the first people I met was a young Puerto Rican of color acting as interpreter for the Loyalist troops.

A few days later in Valencia, I came across two intelligent young colored men from the West Indies, aviators, who had come to give their services to the fight against Fascism.

And now, in Madrid, Spain's besieged capital, I've met wide-awake Negroes from various parts of the world—New York, our Middle West, the French West Indies, Cuba, Africa—some stationed here, others on leave from their battalions—all of them here because they know that if Fascism creeps across Spain, across Europe, and then across the world, there will be no place left for intelligent young Negroes at all. In fact, no decent place for any Negroes—because Fascism preaches the creed of Nordic supremacy and a world for whites alone.

In Spain, there is no color prejudice. Here in Madrid, heroic and bravest of cities, Madrid where the shells of Franco plow through the roof-tops at night, Madrid where you can take a streetcar to the trenches, this Madrid to whose defense lovers of freedom and democracy all over the world have sent food and money and men—here to this Madrid have come Negroes from all the world to offer their help.

On the opposite side of the trenches with Franco, in the company of the professional soldiers of Germany, and the illiterate troops of Italy, are the deluded and driven Moors of North Africa. An oppressed colonial people of color being used by Fascism to make a colony of Spain. And they are being used ruthlessly, without pity. Young boys, men from the desert, old men, and even women, compose the Moorish hordes brought by the reactionaries from Africa to Europe in their attempt to crush the Spanish people.

I did not know about the Moorish women until, a few days ago, I went to visit a prison hospital here in Madrid filled with wounded prisoners. There were German aviators that bombarded the peaceful village of Colmenar Viejo and machine-gunned helpless women as they fled along the road. One of these aviators spoke English. I asked him why he fired on women and children. He said he was a professional soldier who did what he was told. In another ward, there were Italians who joined the invasion of Spain because they had no jobs at home.

But of all the prisoners, I was most interested in the Moors, who are my own color. Some of them, convalescent, in their white wrappings and their bandages, moved silently like dark shadows down the hall. Others lay quietly suffering in their beds. It was difficult to carry on any sort of conversation with them because they spoke little or no Spanish. But finally, we came across a small boy who had been wounded at the battle of Brunete—he looked to be a child of ten or eleven, a bright smiling child who spoke some Spanish.

"Where did you come from?", I said.

He named a town in Morocco I could not understand.

"And how old are you?"

"Thirteen," he said.

"And how did you happen to be fighting in Spain?"

Then I learned from this child that Franco had brought Moorish women into Spain as well as men—women to wash and cook for the troops.

"What happened to your mother," I said.

The child closed his eyes. "She was killed at Brunete," he answered slowly.

Thus the Moors die in Spain, men, women, and children, victims of Fascism, fighting not for freedom—but against freedom—under a banner that holds only terror and segregation for all the darker peoples of the earth.

A great many Negroes know better. Someday the Moors will know better, too. All the Francos in the world cannot blow out the light of human freedom.

The Volunteer for Liberty, September 13, 1937

MADRID—1937

Damaged by shells, many of the clocks on the public buildings in Madrid have stopped. At night, the streets are pitch dark.

—*NEWS ITEM*

Put out the lights and stop the clocks.
Let time stand still,
Again man mocks himself
And all his human will to build and grow.
    Madrid!
The fact and symbol of man's woe.
    Madrid!
Time's end and throw-back,
Birth of darkness,
Years of light reduced:
The ever minus of the brute,
The nothingness of barren land
And stone and metal,

Emptiness of gold,
The dullness of a bill of sale:
BOUGHT AND PAID FOR! SOLD!
Stupidity of hours that do not move
Because all clocks are stopped.
Blackness of nights that do not see
Because all lights are out.
    Madrid!
Beneath the bullets!
    Madrid!
Beneath the bombing planes!
    Madrid!
In the fearful dark!

Oh, mind of man!
So long to make a light
Of fire,
    of oil,
        of gas,
And now electric rays.
So long to make a clock
Of sun-dial,
    sand-dial,
        figures,
And now two hands that mark the hours.
Oh, mind of man!
So long to struggle upward out of darkness
To a measurement of time—
And now:
These guns,
These brainless killers in the Guadarrama hills
Trained on Madrid
To stop the clocks in the towers
And shatter all their faces
Into a million bits of nothingness
In the city
That will not bow its head
To darkness and to greed again:
That dares to dream a cleaner dream!
Oh, mind of man
Moulded into a metal shell—
Left-overs of the past
That rain dull hell and misery
On the world again—

Have your way
And stop the clocks!
Bomb out the lights!
And mock yourself!
Mock all the rights of those
Who live like decent folk.
Let guns alone salute
The wisdom of our age
With dusty powder marks
On yet another page of history.
Let there be no sense of time,
Nor measurement of light and dark,
In fact, no light at all!
Let mankind fall
Into the deepest pit that ignorance can dig
For us all!
Descent is quick.
To rise again is slow.
In the darkness of her broken clocks
Madrid cries NO!
In the timeless midnight of the Fascist guns,
Madrid cries NO!
To all the killers of man's dreams,
Madrid cries NO!

    To break that NO apart
    Will be to break the human heart.

          Madrid, September 24, 1937.

Unpublished poem. Inscribed: "To Arthur Spingarn, Sincerely, Langston."
The Arthur B. Spingarn Papers, Moorland-Spingarn Collection, Howard
University Library.

LAUGHTER IN MADRID

MADRID, DECEMBER 15
The thing about living in Madrid these days is that you
never know when a shell is going to fall or where. Any time is
firing time for Franco. Imagine yourself sitting calmly in the
front room of your third-floor apartment carefully polishing
your eyeglasses when all of a sudden, without the least warn-
ing, a shell decides to come through the wall—paying no atten-
tion to the open window—and explodes like a thunder clap
beneath the sofa. If you are sitting on the sofa, you are out of

luck. If you are at the other side of the room and good at dodging shrapnel you may not be killed. Maybe nobody will even be injured in your apartment. Perhaps the shell will simply go on through the floor and kill somebody else in apartment 27, downstairs. (People across the hall have been killed.)

Who next? Where? When? Today all the shells may fall in the Puerta del Sol. Tomorrow Franco's big guns on the hills outside Madrid may decide to change their range-finders and bombard the city fan-wise, sending *quince-y-medios* from one side of the town to the other. No matter in what section of the city you live, a shell may land in the kitchen of the sixth-floor apartment (whose inhabitants you've often passed on the stairs), penetrate several floors, and make its way to the street via your front room on the third floor.

That explains why practically nobody in Madrid bothers to move when the big guns are heard. If you move, you may as likely as not move into the wrong place. A few days ago four shells went through the walls of the Hotel Florida, making twenty that have fallen there. The entrance to the hotel is well protected with sandbags, but they couldn't sandbag nine stories. All this the desk clerk carefully explains to guests who wish to register. But most of the other hotels have been severely bombed, too. And one has to stay somewhere.

The Hotel Alfonso a few blocks away has several large holes through each of its four walls but is still receiving guests. One of the halls on an upper floor leads straight out into space—door and balcony have been shot away. In one of the unused bedrooms you can look slantingly down three floors into the street through the holes made by a shell that struck the roof and plowed its way down, then out by a side wall into the road. Walking up to your room, you pass a point where the marble stairs are splintered and the wall pitted by scraps of iron; here two people were killed. Yet the Hotel Alfonso maintains its staff, and those of its rooms that still have walls and windows are occupied by paying guests.

The now world-famous Telefonica, Madrid's riddled skyscraper in the center of the city, is still standing, proud but ragged, its telephone girls at work inside. The Madrid Post Office has no window-panes left whatsoever, but the mail still goes out. Around the Cibeles Fountain in front of the Post Office the streetcars still pass although the fountain itself with its lovely goddess is now concealed by a specially built housing of bricks and sandbags, so that the good-natured

Madrileños have nicknamed it "Beauty Under Covers," laughing at their own wit.

Yes, people still laugh in Madrid. In this astonishing city of bravery and death, where the houses run right up to the trenches and some of the streetcar lines stop only at the barricades, people still laugh, children play in the streets, and men buy comic papers as well as war news. The shell holes of the night before are often filled in by dawn, so efficient is the wrecking service and so valiantly do the Madrileños struggle to patch up their city.

A million people living on the front lines of a nation at war! The citizens of Madrid—what are they like? Not long ago a small shell fell in the study of a bearded professor of ancient languages. Frantically his wife and daughter came running to see if anything had happened to him. They found him standing in the center of the floor, holding the shell and shaking his head quizzically. "This little thing," he said, "this inanimate object, can't do us much damage. It's the philosophy that lies behind it, wife, the philosophy that lies behind it."

In the Arguelles quarter to the north, nearest to the rebel lines—the neighborhood that has suffered most from bombardments and air raids—many of the taller apartment houses, conspicuous targets that they are, have been abandoned. But in the smaller houses of one and two stories people still live and go about their tasks. The Cuban poet, Alejo Carpentier, told me that one morning after a heavy shelling he passed a house of which part of the front wall was lying in the yard. A shell had passed through the roof, torn away part of the wall, carried with it the top of the family piano. and buried itself in the garden. Nevertheless, there at the piano sat the young daughter of the house, very clean and starched, her hair brushed and braided, her face shining. Diligently she was beating out a little waltz from a· music book in front of her. The fact that the top of the piano had been shot away in the night did not seem to affect the chords. When passers-by asked about it, calling through the shell hole, the child said, "Yes, an *obús* came right through here last night. I'm going to help clean up the yard after a while, but I have to practice my lessons now. My music teacher'll be here at eleven."

The will to live and laugh in Madrid is the thing that constantly amazes a stranger. At the house where I am staying, sometimes a meal consists largely of bread and of soup made

with bread. Everybody tightens his belt and grins, and some-
body is sure to repeat good-naturedly an old Spanish saying,
"Bread with bread—food for fools!" Then we all laugh.

One of Franco's ways of getting back at Madrid is to broad-
cast daily from his radio stations at Burgos and Seville the
luncheon and dinner menus of the big hotels, the fine food
that the Fascists are eating and the excellent wines they
drink. (Rioja and the best of wine areas are in Fascist hands.)
But Madrid has ways of getting even with the Fascists, too.
Mola, a lover of cafes, said at the very beginning of the war
that he would soon be drinking coffee in Madrid. He was mis-
taken. Then he said he would enter Madrid by the first of No-
vember. He didn't. Then he swore he would enter the city on
the eighth of December. He didn't. But on the evening of the
eighth some wag remembered, and the crowds passing that
night in Madrid's darkened Puerta del Sol saw by moonlight
in the very center of the square a coffee table, carefully set, the
coffee poured, and neatly pinned to the white cloth a large
sign reading "For Mola."

Bread and coffee are scarce in Madrid, and so are cigarettes.
The only cigarettes offered for sale more or less regularly are
small, hard, and very bad. They are so bad that though they
cost thirty centimos before the war they bring only twenty
now despite their comparative scarcity. The soldiers call them
"recruit-killers," jocularly asserting that they are as dangerous
to the new men in the army as are bombs and bullets.

Bad cigarettes, poor wine, little bread, no soap, no sugar!
Madrid, dressed in bravery and laughter; knowing death and
the sound of guns by day and night, but resolved to live, not
die!

The moving-picture theaters are crowded. Opening late in
the afternoon and compelled to close at nine, they give only
one or two showings a day. One evening an audience was fol-
lowing with great interest an American film. Suddenly an
obús fell in the street outside. There was a tremendous deto-
nation, but nobody moved from his seat. The film went on.
Soon another fell, nearer and louder than before, shaking the
whole building. The manager went out into the lobby and
looked up and down the Gran Via. Overhead he heard the
whine of shells. He went inside and mounted the stage to say
that, in view of the shelling, he thought it best to stop the pic-
ture. Before he had got the words out of his mouth he was
greeted with such a hissing and booing and stamping of feet

and calls for the show to go on that he shrugged his shoulders in resignation and signaled the operator to continue. The house was darkened. The magic of Hollywood resumed its spell. While Franco's shells whistled dangerously over the theater, the film went its make-believe way to a thrilling dénouement. The picture was called "Terror in Chicago."

The Nation, January 29, 1938

AIR RAID: BARCELONA

Black smoke of sound
Curls against the midnight sky.
Deeper than a whistle,
Louder than a cry,
Worse than a scream
Tangled in the wail
Of a nightmare dream,
   The siren
Of the air raid sounds.

Flames and bombs and
Death in the ear!
The siren announces
Planes drawing near.
Down from bedrooms
Stumble women in gowns.
Men, half-dressed,
Carrying children rush down.
Up in the sky-lanes
Against the stars
A flock of death birds
Whose wings are steel bars
Fill the sky with a low dull roar
Of a plane,
   two planes,
      three planes,
         five planes,
            or more.
The anti-aircraft guns bark into space.
The searchlights make wounds
On the night's dark face.
The siren's wild cry
Like a hollow scream

Echoes out of hell in a nightmare dream
   Then the BOMBS fall!
All other noises are nothing at all
   When the first BOMBS fall.
All other noises are suddenly still
   When the BOMBS fall
All other noises are deathly still
As blood spatters the wall
And the whirling sound
Of the iron star of death
Comes hurtling down.
No other noises can be heard
As a child's life goes up
In the night like a bird.
Swift pursuit planes
Dart over the town,
Steel bullets fly
Slitting the starry silk
   Of the sky:
A bomber's brought down
In flames orange and blue,
And the night's all red
Like blood, too.
   The last BOMB falls.

The death birds wheel East
To their lairs again
Leaving iron eggs
In the streets of Spain.
With wings like black cubes
Against the far dawn,
The stench of their passage
Remains when they're gone.
In what was a courtyard
A child weeps alone.

Men uncover bodies
From ruins of stone.

Esquire, October 1938

MOONLIGHT IN VALENCIA: CIVIL WAR

Moonlight in Valencia:
The moon meant planes.

The planes meant death.
And not heroic death.
Like death on a poster:
An officer in a pretty uniform
Or a nurse in a clean white dress—
But death with steel in your brain,
Powder burns on your face,
Blood spilling from your entrails,
And you didn't laugh
Because there was no laughter in it.
You didn't cry PROPAGANDA either.
The propaganda was too much
For everybody concerned.
It hurt you to your guts.
It was real
As anything you ever saw
In the movies:
Moonlight. . . .
Me cago en la ostia!
Bombers over
Valencia.

Seven Poets in Search of an Answer, ed., Thomas Yoseloff, New York, Bernard Ackerman, 1944, p. 51.

TOMORROW'S SEED

Proud banners of death
I see them waving
There against the sky,
Struck deep in Spanish earth
Where your dark bodies lie
Inert and helpless—
So they think
Who do not know
That from your death
New life will grow.
For there are those who cannot see
The mighty roots of liberty
Push upward in the dark
To burst in flame—
A million stars—
And one your name:
      Man

Who fell in Spanish earth:
Human seed
For freedom's birth.

The Heart of Spain, ed., Alvah Bessie, Veterans of the Abraham Lincoln Brigade, 1952, p. 325.

HERO—INTERNATIONAL BRIGADE

Blood,
Or a flag,
Or a flame
Or life itself
Are they the same:
Our dream?
      I came.
An ocean in-between
And half a continent.
Frontiers,
And mountains skyline tall,
And governments that told me NO,
YOU CANNOT GO!
I came.
On tomorrow's bright frontiers
I placed the strength and wisdom
Of my years.
Not much,
For I am young.
(*Was* young,
Perhaps it's better said—
For now I'm dead.)

But had I lived four score and ten
Life could not've had
A better end.
I've given what I wished
And what I had to give
That others live.
And when the bullets
Cut my heart away,
And the blood
Gushed to my throat
I wondered if it were blood
Gushing there.
Or a red flame?

Or just my death
Turned into life?
They're all the same
Our dream!
     My death!
     Your life!
     Our blood!
     One flame!
They're all the same!

The Heart of Spain, ed., Alvah Bessie, Veterans of the Abraham Lincoln Brigade, 1952, pp. 325-326.

11
CHINA

THE REVOLUTIONARY ARMIES IN CHINA—1949

What is happening in China is important to Negroes, in fact, to people of color all around the world, because each time an old bastion of white supremacy crumbles its falling weakens the whole Jim Crow system everywhere. Under the Nationalist government in China with its white western backers, there was a great deal of Jim Crow. I saw it with my own eyes in Shanghai and Nanking when I was there before the war. Being colored, I felt it, too. I do not like Jim Crow in either Chicago or China. The majority of Chinese people did not like Jim Crow either. But the Chinese Uncle Toms like Jim Crow because they grew rich from it. Chiang Kai-shek was a Chinese Uncle Tom.

Emerging slowly from feudalism with large sections of the country dominated by war-lords, China has long had slavery—child-slavery, woman-slavery, "white-slavery." From this ancient slavery white westerners have long profited along with the rich Chinese. Factories in which children purchased from their parents at an early age worked twelve and fifteen hours a day under guards brought huge profits to foreign and Chinese investors alike. Child prostitution and the dope rackets profited people in far off London and Paris. Our own United States, with large investments in China, supported the Chiang Kai-shek regime that permitted these antiquated and inhuman exploitations to exist.

I am not speaking of what I have read. I am speaking of what I saw myself in China. With American Y.W.C.A. workers I visited factories in Shanghai where children of eight to twelve worked from dawn to dusk under overseers who carried bamboo canes to throttle them if they became idle. I saw the miserable dormitories where these purchased children slept in virtual imprisonment. And I was told that wealthy and respectable stock-holders in far off Tokyo and London and New York and Paris lived on the dividends produced by the frail hands of these children.

In Shanghai's International Settlement where the great powers of the world had their consulates and their laws and their police, I saw in the amusement centers children with guardians, not there to enjoy themselves, but rather offered in prostitution to any wishing to pay the fee asked by their "nurses." American newspaper men explained to me that often very poor parents sold their offspring into this horrible business rather than see them starve.

Quite openly in Shanghai before the war one might see a white foreigner curse or even strike a rickshaw driver—the rickshaws being the human taxis of the East pulled by a man running, running, running all the time. No policeman would arrest a white foreigner for striking a rickshaw man—just as no policeman would arrest a white man for striking a Negro in parts of Mississippi or Georgia today.

In Shanghai when I was there, there was a big Y.M.C.A. building for whites and a kind of "Harlem" Branch, separate and elsewhere, for Chinese and other colored peoples. There were, right in China's greatest city, many hotels and restaurants for EUROPEANS ONLY, which meant WHITE ONLY. Such was the nerve of the western powers in the Far East before the Japanese invaded the mainland of Asia! The Japanese swept the color-line out of existence. But the Japanese did not sweep away exploitation and child-labor. That is why the revolutionary armies now sweeping over China are doing a better job. They are not only against color-lines and Jim Crow. They are also against child-labor, child-prostitution, dope-rackets with headquarters in Europe, and dividend collectors who grow rich in far away lands from the dawn to dusk hours of Chinese workers.

Title supplied by the editor.

The Chicago Defender, October 8, 1949

Roar China!

Roar, China!
Roar, old lion of the East!
Snort fire, yellow dragon of the Orient,
Tired at last of being bothered.
Since when did you ever steal anything
From anybody,
Sleepy wise old beast
Known as the porcelain-maker,
Known as the poem-maker,
Known as maker of firecrackers?
A long time since you cared
About taking other people's lands
Away from them.
THEY must've thought you didn't care
About your own land either—
So THEY came with gunboats,

Set up Concessions,
Zones of influence,
International Settlements,
Missionary houses,
Banks,
And Jim Crow Y.M.C.A.'s.
THEY beat you with malacca canes
And dared you to raise your head—
Except to cut it off.
Even the yellow men came
To take what the white men
Hadn't already taken.
The yellow men dropped bombs on Chapei.
The yellow men called you the same names
The white men did:

> *Dog! Dog! Dog!*
> *Coolie dog!*
> *Red! . . . Lousy red!*
> *Red coolie dog!*

And in the end you had no place
To make your porcelain,
Write your poems,
Or shoot your firecrackers on holidays.
In the end you had no peace
Or calm left at all.
PRESIDENT, KING, MIKADO
Thought you really were a dog.
THEY kicked you daily
Via radiophone, via cablegram,
Via gunboats in the harbor,
Via malacca canes.
THEY thought you were a tame lion.
A sleepy, easy, tame old lion!

> Ha! Ha!
> Haaa-aa-a! . . . Ha!

Laugh, little coolie boy on the docks of Shanghai, laugh!
> You're no tame lion.
Laugh, red generals in the hills of Siang-kiang, laugh!
> You're no tame lion.
Laugh, child slaves in the factories of the foreigners!
> You're no tame lion.
Laugh—and roar, China! Time to spit fire!
Open your mouth, old dragon of the East,

To swallow up the gunboats in the Yangtse!
Swallow up the foreign planes in your sky!
Eat bullets, old maker of firecrackers—
And spit out freedom in the face of your enemies!
Break the chains of the East,
    Little coolie boy!
Break the chains of the East,
    Red generals!
Break the chains of the East,
    Child slaves in the factories!
Smash the iron gates of the Concessions!
Smash the pious doors of the missionary houses!
Smash the revolving doors of the Jim Crow Y.M.C.A.'s.
Crush the enemies of land and bread and freedom!
    Stand up and roar, China!
    You know what you want!
    The only way to get it is
    To take it!
    Roar, China!

The Volunteer for Liberty, August 30, 1937

CONCERNING THE FUTURE OF ASIA

In a recent issue of *The New York Times* four of the eight columns constituting its front page were devoted to events in Asia. The entire second page, except for the ads and a very small news item of a dozen lines, was also given over to Asian news—India, Korea, Cambodia. About half the third page, too, concerned Asia—China, Vietnam, the Calcutta riots. Most of the space on the all first three pages of America's leading newspaper that day was devoted to the darker world, primarily Asia. Well might the white world pay a great deal of attention to Asia. Its future lies there.

What is happening, and has happened in Asia, certainly affects the political thinking and official behavior in the United States today. Fortunately, by and large, it affects this behavior for the better. The old arrogance in public utterances toward the Asian world is disappearing. There is pique, yes, at the new spirit of independence in the countries of the East. But there is no longer the same contempt there once was among our American white folks.

Since the major portion of American radio and TV dramas are built around force and violence, and many of our most successful movies extol it— "Shane" being a current example where problems are solved not by taking thought but by gun-fire and uppercuts—it may be that Asian toughness on the field of battle is what has brought about this new American semblance of respect. Certainly Japan shook the white world to its very roots at Pearl Harbor. The Dutch were no military match for the Indonesians. Red China told everybody to kiss her unbound feet.

And after months of blood and battle, we still did not get to the Yalu River in Korea. It was Asian colored folks who pro-voked America into dropping the first atom bomb ever used on human beings on this earth. And *The New York Herald Tribune* recently reported, "It is known that the Pentagon for some time had plans ready for the use of atomic weapons in Korea."

I think it would be a very great mistake for the white world to drop another atom bomb anywhere across the Pacific. I think it would only step up the beginning of that world's end and insofar as military or moral power goes. Of course, the white world may HAVE to drop an atom bomb in Asia to find this out, since a sense of reality and reason seems alien to a large portion of our officialdom. There are some very stupid men in the capitals of the Western World—the more stupid because they think they are so wise. It would seem to me that almost anybody would know by now that colored peoples do not like to be ruled by outside forces, Jim Crowed, segregated, told what to do by aliens, and in general kicked around. It would also seem to me that almost anybody could see, just by reading the papers, that modern Asia does not mind fighting and dying to achieve independence, or to keep it once it is achieved. *The New York Times* says as much almost every day. Returning travellers from the Orient all affirm it.

In a brilliantly written article in *The New York Times Magazine* of Sunday, June 28th [1953], called "The Greatest Power in Asia is the People," Chester Bowles, our former Am-bassador to India, says, "For better or for worse, the ability of the Asian people to guide their own future is firmly estab-lished. The West can persuade but it can no longer com-mand." He names as one of the great aims of Asia, "their aspi-rations to achieve equal status as human beings with the white people of the West." He continues, "The objective of the Asian revolution may be said to be: national indepen-dence, improved economic opportunities, and human dignity, concepts which few Americans will disapprove." I wish Chester Bowles had inserted after the word "few" the word "decent"—since there are still a great many Americans who cannot see their way clear to granting human dignity to the millions of Negro citizens in the United States, much less to folks way over in Asia. The Negro problem is one thing that makes it so hard for them to look clearly at Asia, because their racial specs are still very cloudy at home.

The New York Times does not report as fully on the colored American scene as it does on colored Asia. But every issue of the great Negro newspapers carry stories of American Negro citizens who have to struggle all the way up to the United States Supreme Court, investing great sums of money and much time and heartache, to even stay in a house they have bought with their hard-earned cash, or to buy a cup of coffee in a public place, or send their children to a decent school, or get on a jury, or have a fair trial, or to protect themselves from the excessive use of police clubs. Until these little problems are settled right here at home, it is going to be very hard for some Americans not to think that the easiest way to settle the problems of Asia is by simply dropping an atom bomb on colored heads there. I wish, for all our sakes, they could realize that things are not that simple.

Title supplied by the editor.

The Chicago Defender, August 15, 1953

12

THE AMERICAN WRITERS'
CONGRESS

The American Writers' Congress was organized in early 1935, with the support of over 200 authors, including Nelson Algren, Van Wyck Brooks, Erskine Caldwell, Malcolm Cowley, Theodore Dreiser, James Farrell, Waldo Frank, Josephine Herbst, Granville Hicks, Langston Hughes, James Weldon Johnson, Lincoln Steffens and Richard Wright. A forum for militant causes, the Congress held four national conferences in New York City in 1935, 1937, 1939 and 1941. The first Congress established its own organization, the League of American Writers, "a voluntary association of writers dedicated to the preservation and extension of a truly democratic culture." The League was an affiliate of the International Association of Writers for the Defense of Culture which met at congresses in London (1936), Madrid (1937), and Paris (1938). Hughes, elected one of seven vice presidents of the League in 1937, remained one of its most active supporters until the organization was dissolved in 1942. His speeches to the first and third national sessions of the American Writers' Congress are included here.

To Negro Writers*

*The speech made by Langston Hughes at the Public Session of the First American Writers' Congress, Mecca Temple, New York City, April, 1935.

There are certain practical things American Negro writers can do through their work.

We can reveal to the Negro masses from which we come, our potential power to transform the now ugly face of the Southland into a region of peace and plenty.

We can reveal to the white masses those Negro qualities which go beyond the mere ability to laugh and sing and dance and make music, and which are a part of the useful heritage that we place at the disposal of a future free America.

Negro writers can seek to unite blacks and whites in our country, not on the nebulous basis of an interracial meeting, or the shifting sands of religious brotherhood, but on the *solid* ground of the daily working-class struggle to wipe out, now and forever, all the old inequalities of the past.

Furthermore, by way of exposure, Negro writers can reveal in their novels, stories, poems, and articles:

The lovely grinning face of Philanthropy—which gives a million dollars to a Jim Crow school, but not one job to a graduate of that school; which builds a Negro hospital with second-rate equipment, then commands black patients and stu-dent-doctors to go there whether they will or no; or which, out of the kindness of its heart, erects yet another separate, segregated, shut-off, Jim Crow Y.M.C.A.

Negro writers can expose those white labor leaders who keep their unions closed against Negro workers and prevent the betterment of all workers.

We can expose, too, the sick-sweet smile of organized reli-gion—which lies about what it doesn't know, and about what it *does* know. And the half-voodoo, half-clown, face of revival-ism, dulling the mind with the clap of its empty hands.

Expose, also, the false leadership that besets the Negro peo-ple—bought and paid for leadership, owned by capital, afraid to open its mouth except in the old conciliatory way so advan-tageous to the exploiters.

And all the economic roots of race hatred and race fear.

And the Contentment Tradition of the O-lovely-Negroes school of American fiction, which makes an ignorant black face and a Carolina head filled with superstition, appear more desirable than a crown of gold; the jazz-band; and the O-sogay writers who make of the Negro's poverty and misery a dusky funny paper.

And expose war. And the old My-Country-'Tis-of-Thee lie. And the colored American Legion posts strutting around talking about the privilege of dying for the noble Red, White and Blue, when they aren't even permitted the privilege of living for it. Or voting for it in Texas. Or working for it in the diplomatic service. Or even rising, like every other good little boy, from the log cabin to the White House.

White House is right.

Dear colored American Legion, you can swing from a lynching tree, uniform and all, with pleasure—and nobody'll fight for you. Don't you know that? Nobody even salutes you down South, dead or alive, medals or no medals, chevrons or not, no matter how many wars you've fought in.

Let Negro writers write about the irony and pathos of the *colored* American Legion.

"*Salute, Mr. White Man!*"

"Salute, hell! . . . You're a nigger."

Or would you rather write about the moon?

Sure, the moon still shines over Harlem. Shines over Scottsboro. Shines over Birmingham, too, I reckon. Shines over Cordie Cheek's grave, down South.

Write about the moon if you want to. Go ahead. This is a free country.

But there are certain very practical things American Negro writers can do. And must do. There's a song that says, "the time ain't long." That song is right. Something has got to change in America—and change soon. We must help that change to come.

The moon's still shining as poetically as ever, but all the stars on the flag are dull. (And the stripes, too.)

We want a new and better America, where there won't be any poor, where there won't be any more Jim Crow, where there won't be any lynchings, where there won't be any munition makers, where we won't need philanthropy, nor charity, nor the New Deal, nor Home Relief.

We want an America that will be ours, a world that will be ours—we Negro workers and white workers! Black writers and white!

We'll make that world!

American Writers' Congress, ed., Henry Hart, New York, International Publishers, 1935, pp. 139-141.

DEMOCRACY AND ME*

*The speech made by Langston Hughes at the Public Session of the Third American Writers' Congress, Carnegie Hall, New York City, June, 1939.

Twice now I have had the honor and the pleasure of representing the League of American Writers at Congresses held abroad in Paris and in Spain. In Europe I spoke first as an American and as a writer, and secondarily as a Negro. Tonight, here in New York at the Third American Writers' Congress, I feel it wise in the interest of democracy to reverse the order, and to speak first as a Negro and a writer, and secondarily as an American—because Negroes are secondary Americans. All the problems known to the Jews today in Hitler's Germany, we who are Negroes know here in America—with one difference. Here we may speak openly about our problems, write about them, protest, and seek to better our conditions. In Germany the Jews may do none of these things. Democracy permits us the freedom of a hope, and some action towards the realization of that hope. Because we live in a democracy, tonight I may stand here and talk to you about our common problem, the problem of democracy and me.

Since this a Writers' Congress, I shall approach that problem as a writer. I shall speak of the color-line as it affects writers, as it affects me—and when I say me, I do not mean me, myself, alone. By me, I mean all those Negro writers who are seeking to put on paper today in the form of verse, or prose, or drama, life in America as we know it.

Here are our problems: In the first place, Negro books are considered by editors and publishers as *exotic*. Negro material is placed, like Chinese material or Bali material or East Indian material, into a certain classification. Magazine editors will tell you, "We can use but so many Negro stories a year." (That "so many" meaning very few.) Publishers will say, "We already have one Negro novel on our list this fall."

The market for Negro writers, then, is definitely limited as long as we write about ourselves. And the more truthfully we write about ourselves, the more limited our market becomes. Those novels about Negroes that sell best, by Negroes or whites, those novels that make the best-seller lists and receive the leading prizes, are almost always books that touch very lightly upon the facts of Negro life, books that make our black ghettos in the big cities seem very happy places indeed, and our plantations in the deep South idyllic in their pastoral loveliness. In such books there is no hunger and no segregation, no lynchings and no fears, no intimidations and no Jim Crow. The exotic is the quaint and the happy—the pathetic or melodramatic, perhaps, but not the tragic. We are considered exotic. When we cease to be exotic, we do not sell well.

I know, of course, that very few writers of any race make a living directly from their writing. You must be very lucky and very famous to do that. But a great many American writers—who are not Negroes—may make a living in fields more or less connected with writing. They may thus be professional writers living on or from their literary reputations and able, from their earnings, to afford some leisure time for personal creation. Whether their books are good or bad, they may work in editorial offices, on publishers' staffs, in publicity firms, in radio, or in motion pictures. Practically never is such employment granted to a Negro writer though he be as famous as the late James Weldon Johnson or as excellent a craftsman as the living Richard Wright. Perhaps an occasional prize or a fellowship may come a Negro writer's way—but not a job. It is very hard for a Negro to become a professional writer. Magazine offices, daily newspapers, publishers' offices are as tightly closed to us in America as if we were pure non-Aryans in Berlin.

Of course, Negro novelists do not sell their novels to motion pictures. No motion picture studio in America, in all the history of motion pictures, has yet dared make one single picture using any of the fundamental dramatic values of Negro life—not one. Not one picture. On the screen we are servants, clowns, or fools. Comedy relief. Droll and very funny. Such Negro material as is used by the studios is very rarely written by Negroes.

I speak first of this problem of earning a living because it is basic. Most undernourished writers die young—or cease to be writers, because they are forced to do something else.

Let us turn to the lecture field, a source of income for many Nordic and non-Nordic writers who are white. The leading lecture bureaus do not handle Negro speakers. Thousands of women's clubs and forums have never had—and will not have —a Negro speaker. Since tea is often served, the factor of social equality, of course, enters into the arrangements. In a number of states of our American republic, it is prohibited by law for whites and Negroes to drink tea together in public places.

On lecture tour, the Negro writer, if a tour he has, runs

into all the difficulties that beset colored travellers everywhere in this country: in the South the Jim Crow coach and the segregated waiting room. If travelling by car, no tourist camps for Negroes, few restaurants that will serve a meal. Everywhere lack of hotel accommodations. This week the press reports that Marian Anderson was refused accommodations in the Hotel Lincoln at Springfield [Illinois] where she went to sing at the premiere of *Young Mr. Lincoln.* Negro writers and artists on tour in this country, if greeted with acclaim on the platform, are often rudely received outside the hall as human beings. They are expected, I suppose, to sleep in stables, if there happen to be no colored families in the town to accommodate them.

Ten days ago, a friend of mine, a well-known Negro novelist whose third novel has just come from the press, was invited to talk about his book before a large women's club at their clubhouse. At the hour of the lecture, the novelist could not get past the attendant at the outer door. He was forced to go to the corner drugstore and telephone the ladies that he was on the sidewalk waiting to appear before them. Doormen, you see, and elevator operators accustomed to our segregation patterns, will often not admit Negroes to hotels and clubs even when they say they are specifically invited there as guests. Negroes, in America, whether they be authors or not, are still expected to use the servant's entrance.

When these things are put into a story or book, they are not exotic or charming. There is about them no sweet southern humor—even when told in dialect—so they do not sell well. One of our oldest and most cultural of American magazines once, in turning down a story of mine—which they had a perfect right to turn down on literary grounds—wrote me a quaint little note with it. The editor said, "We believe our readers still read for pleasure."

So, in summary: The market for Negro writers is very limited. Jobs as professional writers, editorial assistants, publisher's readers, etc., are almost non-existent. Hollywood insofar as Negroes are concerned, might just as well be controlled by Hitler. The common courtesies of decent travel, hotel and restaurant accommodations, politeness from doormen, elevatormen, and hired attendants in public places is practically everywhere in America denied Negroes, whether they be writers or not. Black authors, too, must ride in Jim Crow cars.

These are some of our problems. What can you who are

writers do to help us solve them? What can you, our public, do to help us solve them? My problem, your problem. No, I'm wrong! It is not a matter of *mine* and *yours*. It is a matter of *ours*. We are all Americans. We want to create the American dream, a finer and more democratic America. I cannot do it without you. You cannot do it omitting me. Can we march together then?

But perhaps the word *march* is the wrong word—suggesting soldiers and armies. Can we not put our heads together and think and plan—not merely dream—the future America? And then create it with our hands? A land where even a Negro writer can make a living, if he is a good writer. And where, being a Negro, he need not be a secondary American.

We do not want any secondary Americans. We do not want a weak and imperfect democracy. We do not want poverty and hunger and prejudice and fear on the part of any portion of our population. We want America to really be America for everybody. Let us make it so!

The Bancroft Library, University of California, Berkeley

Excerpts of this speech originally appeared in *Fighting Words,* ed., Donald Ogden Stewart, New York, Harcourt Brace & Co., 1940, pp. 58-63.

13
RETROSPECTIVE

Concerning "Goodbye, Christ"

Almost ten years ago now, I wrote a poem in the form of a dramatic monologue entitled "Goodbye, Christ" with the intention in mind of shocking into being in religious people a consciousness of the admitted shortcomings of the church in regard to the condition of the poor and oppressed of the world, particularly the Negro people.

Just previous to the writing of the poem, in 1931 I had made a tour through the heart of our American Southland. For the first time I saw peonage, million-dollar high schools for white children and shacks for Negro children (both of whose parents work and pay taxes and are Americans). I saw vast areas in which Negro citizens were not permitted to vote, I saw the Scottsboro boys in prison in Alabama and colored citizens of the state afraid to utter a word in their defense, I crossed rivers by ferry where the Negro drivers of cars had to wait until all the white cars behind them had been accommodated before boarding the ferry even if it meant missing the boat. I motored as far North as Seattle and back across America to New York through towns and cities where neither bed nor board was to be had if you were colored, cafes, hotels, and tourist camps were closed to all non-whites. I saw the horrors of hunger and unemployment among my people in the segregated ghettos of our great cities. I saw lecture halls and public cultural institutions closed to them. I saw the Hollywood caricatures of what pass for Negroes on the screens that condition the attitudes of a nation. I visited state and religious colleges to which no Negroes were admitted. To me these things appeared unbelievable in a Christian country. Had not Christ said, "Such as ye do unto the least of these, ye do it unto Me."? But almost nobody seemed to care. Sincere Christians seeking to combat this condition were greatly in the minority.

Directly from this extensive tour of America, I went to the Soviet Union. There it seemed to me that Marxism had put into practical being many of the precepts which our own Christian America had not yet been able to bring to life, for, in the Soviet Union, meagre as the resources of the country were, white and black, Asiatic and European, Jew and Gentile stood alike as citizens on an equal footing protected from racial inequalities by the law. There were no pogroms, no lynchings, no Jim Crow cars as there had once been in Tzarist Asia, nor were the newspapers or movies permitted to ridicule or malign any people because of race. I was deeply impressed by these things.

It was then that I wrote "Goodbye, Christ." In the poem I contrasted what seemed to me the declared and forthright position of those who, on the religious side in America (in apparent actions toward my people) had said to Christ and the Christian principles, "Goodbye, beat it on away from here now, you're done for." I gave to such religionists what seemed to me to be their own words merged with the words of the orthodox Marxist who declared he had no further use nor need for religion.

I couched the poem in the language of the first person, I, as many poets have done in the past in writing of various characters other than themselves. The *I* which I pictured was the newly liberated peasant of the state collectives I had seen in Russia merged with those American Negro workers of the depression period who believed in the Soviet dream and the hope it held out for a solution of their racial and economic difficulties. (Just as the *I* pictured in many of my blues poems is the poor and uneducated Negro of the South—and not myself who grew up in Kansas.) At the time that "Goodbye, Christ" first appeared, many persons seemed to think I was the characterized *I* of the poem. Then, as now, they failed to see the poem in connection with my other work, including many verses most sympathetic to the true Christian spirit for which I have always had great respect—such as that section of poems, "Feet Of Jesus," in my book, *The Dream Keeper*, or the chapters on religion in my novel, *Not Without Laughter* which received the Harmon Gold Award from the Federated Council of Churches. They failed to consider "Goodbye, Christ" in the light of various of my other poems in the ironic or satirical vein, such as "Red Silk Stockings"—which some of my critics once took to be literal advice.

Today, accompanied by a sound truck playing "God Bless America" and bearing pickets from the Aimee Semple McPherson Temple of the Four Square Gospel in Los Angeles, my poem of ten years ago is resurrected without my permission and distributed on handbills before a Pasadena Hotel where I was to speak on Negro folk songs. Some weeks later it was reprinted in *The Saturday Evening Post*, a magazine whose columns, like the doors of many of our churches, has been until recently entirely closed to Negroes, and whose chief contribution in the past to a better understanding of Negro life in America has been the Octavius Roy Cohen stories with which most colored people have been utterly disgusted.

Now, in the year 1941, having left the terrain of "the radical at twenty" to approach the "conservative of forty," I would not and could not write "Goodbye, Christ," desiring no longer to *épater le bourgeois*. However, since those at present engaged in distributing my poem do not date it, nor say how long ago it was written, I feel impelled for the benefit of persons reading the poem for the first time, to make the following statement:

"Goodbye, Christ" does not represent my personal viewpoint. It was long ago withdrawn from circulation and has been reprinted recently without my knowledge or consent. I would not now use such a technique of approach since I feel that a mere poem is quite unable to compete in power to shock with the current horrors of war and oppression abroad in the greater part of the world. I have never been a member of the Communist party. Furthermore, I have come to believe that no system of ethics, religion, morals, or government is of permanent value which does not first start with and change the human heart. Mortal frailty, greed, and error, know no boundary lines. The explosives of war do not care whose hands fashion them. Certainly, both Marxists and Christians can be cruel. Would that Christ came back to save us all. We do not know how to save ourselves.

Langston Hughes
January 1, 1941

My Adventures as a Social Poet

Poets who write mostly about love, roses and moonlight, sunsets and snow, must lead a very quiet life. Seldom, I imagine, does their poetry get them into difficulties. Beauty and lyricism are really related to another world, to ivory towers, to your head in the clouds, feet floating off the earth.

Unfortunately, having been born poor—and also colored—in Missouri, I was stuck in the mud from the beginning. Try as I might to float off into the clouds, poverty and Jim Crow would grab me by the heels, and right back on earth I would land. A third-floor furnished room is the nearest thing I have ever had to an ivory tower.

Some of my earliest poems were social poems in that they were about people's problems—whole groups of people's problems—rather than my own personal difficulties. Sometimes, though, certain aspects of my personal problems happened to be also common to many other people. And certainly, racially speaking, my own problems of adjustment to American life were the same as those of millions of other segregated Negroes. The moon belongs to everybody, but not this American earth of ours. That is perhaps why poems about the moon perturb no one, but poems about color and poverty do perturb many citizens. Social forces pull backwards or forwards, right or left, and social poems get caught in the pulling and hauling. Sometimes the poet himself gets pulled and hauled—even hauled off to jail.

I have never been in jail but I have been detained by the Japanese police in Tokyo and by the immigration authorities in Cuba—in custody, to put it politely—due, no doubt, to their interest in my written words. These authorities would hardly have detained me had I been a writer of the roses and moonlight school. I have never known the police of any country to show an interest in lyric poetry as such. But when poems stop talking about the moon and begin to mention poverty, trade unions, color lines, and colonies, somebody tells the police. The history of world literature has many examples of poets fleeing into exile to escape persecution, of poets in jail, even of poets killed like Placido or, more recently, Lorca in Spain.

My adventures as a social poet are mild indeed compared to the body-breaking, soul-searing experiences of poets in the recent Fascist countries or of the resistance poets of the Nazi-invaded lands during the war. For that reason, I can use so light a word as "adventure" in regard to my own skirmishes with reaction and censorship.

My adventures as a social poet began in a colored church in Atlantic City shortly after my first book, *The Weary Blues,* was published in 1926. I had been invited to come down to the shore from Lincoln University where I was a student, to give a program of my poems in the church. During the course of my program I read several of my poems in the form of the Negro folk songs, including some blues poems about hard luck and hard work. As I read I noticed a deacon approach the pulpit with a note which he placed on the rostrum beside me, but I did not stop to open the note until I had finished and had acknowledged the applause of a cordial audience. The note read, "Do not read any more blues in my pulpit." It was signed by the minister. That was my first experience with censorship.

The kind and generous woman who sponsored my writing for a few years after my college days did not come to the point quite so directly as did the minister who disliked blues. Perhaps, had it not been in the midst of the great depression of the late '20's and early '30's, the kind of poems that I am afraid helped to end her patronage might not have been written. But it was impossible for me to travel from hungry Harlem to the lovely homes on Park Avenue without feeling in my soul the great gulf between the very poor and the very rich in our society. In those days, on the way to visit this kind lady I would see the homeless sleeping in subways and the hungry begging in doorways on sleet-stung winter days. It was then that I wrote a poem called "Advertisement for the Waldorf-Astoria," satirizing the slick-paper magazine advertisements of the opening of that de luxe hotel. Also I wrote:

PARK BENCH

I live on a park bench,
You, Park Avenue.
Hell of a distance
Between us two.

I beg a dime for dinner—
You got a butler and maid.
But I'm wakin' up!
Say, ain't you afraid

That I might, just maybe,
In a year or two,
Move on over
To Park Avenue?

In a little while I did not have a patron any more.

But that year I won a prize, the Harmon Gold Award for Literature, which consisted of a medal and four hundred dollars. With the four hundred dollars I went to Haiti. On the way I stopped in Cuba and I was cordially received by the writers and artists. I had written poems about the exploitation of Cuba by the sugar barons and I had translated many poems of Nicolás Guillén such as:

CANE

Negro
In the cane fields.

White man
Above the cane fields
Earth
Beneath the cane fields.
Blood
That flows from us.

This was during the days of the dictatorial Machado regime. Perhaps someone called his attention to these poems and translations because, when I came back from Haiti weeks later, I was not allowed to land in Cuba, but was detained by the immigration authorities at Santiago and put on an island until the American consul came, after three days, to get me off with the provision that I cross the country to Havana and leave Cuban soil at once.

That was my first time being put out of any place. But since that time I have been put out of or barred from quite a number of places, all because of my poetry—not the roses and moonlight poems (which I write, too) but because of poems about poverty, oppression, and segregation. Nine Negro boys in Alabama were on trial for their lives when I got back from Cuba and Haiti. The famous Scottsboro "rape" case was in full session. I visited those boys in the death house at Kilby Prison, and I wrote many poems about them. One of these poems was:

CHRIST IN ALABAMA

Christ is a Nigger,
Beaten and black—
O, bare your back.

Mary is His Mother—
Mammy of the South.
Silence your mouth.

God's His Father—
White Master above,
Grant us your love.

Most holy bastard
Of the bleeding mouth:
Nigger Christ
On the cross of the South.

Contempo, a publication of some of the students at the University of North Carolina, published the poem on its front page on the very day that I was being presented in a program of my poems at the University in Chapel Hill. That evening there were police outside the building in which I spoke, and in the air the rising tension of race that is peculiar to the South. It had been rumored that some of the local citizenry were saying that I should be run out of town, and that one of the sheriffs agreed, saying, "Sure, he ought to be run out! It's bad enough to call Christ a *bastard*. But when he calls him a *nigger,* he's gone too far!"

The next morning a third of my fee was missing when I was handed my check. One of the departments of the university jointly sponsoring my program had refused to come through with its portion of the money. Nevertheless, I remember with pleasure the courtesy and kindness of many of the students and faculty at Chapel Hill and their lack of agreement with the anti-Negro elements of the town. There I began to learn at the University of North Carolina how hard it is to be a white liberal in the South.

It was not until I had been to Russia and around the world as a writer and journalist that censorship and opposition to my poems reached the point of completely preventing me from appearing in public programs on a few occasions. It happened first in Los Angeles shortly after my return from the Soviet Union. I was to have been one of several speakers on a memorial program to be held at the colored branch Y.M.C.A. for a young Negro journalist of the community. At the behest of white higher-ups, no doubt, some reactionary Negro politicians informed the Negro Y.M.C.A. that I was a Communist. The secretary of the Negro Branch Y then informed the committee of young people in charge of the memorial that they could have their program only if I did not appear.

I have never been a Communist, but I soon learned that anyone visiting the Soviet Union and speaking with favor of it upon returning is liable to be so labeled. Indeed when Mrs. Roosevelt, Walter White, and so Christian a lady as Mrs. Bethune who has never been in Moscow, are so labeled, I should hardly be surprised! I wasn't surprised. And the young people's committee informed the Y secretary that since the Y was a public community center which they helped to support, they saw no reason why it should censor their memorial program to the extent of eliminating any speaker.

Since I had been allotted but a few moments on the program, it was my intention simply to read this short poem of mine:

> Dear lovely death
> That taketh all things under wing,
> Never to kill,
> Only to change into some other thing
> This suffering flesh—
> To make it either more or less
> But not again the same,
> Dear lovely death,
> Change is thy other name.

But the Negro branch Y, egged on by the reactionary politicians (whose incomes, incidentally, were allegedly derived largely from gambling houses and other underworld activities), informed the young people's committee that the police would be at the door to prevent my entering the Y on the afternoon of the scheduled program. So when the crowd gathered, the memorial was not held that Sunday. The young people simply informed the audience of the situation and said that the memorial would be postponed until a place could be found where all the participants could be heard. The program was held elsewhere a few Sundays later.

Somebody with malice aforethought (probably the Negro politicians of Uncle Tom vintage) gave the highly publicized California evangelist, Aimee Semple McPherson, a copy of a poem of mine, "Goodbye, Christ." This poem was one of my least successful efforts at poetic communication, in that many persons have misinterpreted it as an anti-Christian poem. I intended it to be just the opposite. Satirical, even ironic, in style, I meant it to be a poem against those whom I felt were misusing religion for worldly or profitable purposes. In the poem I mentioned Aimee Semple McPherson. This apparently made her angry. From her Angelus Temple pulpit she preached against me, saying, "There are many devils among us, but the most dangerous of all is the red devil. And now there comes among us a red devil *in a black skin!*"

She gathered her followers together and sent them to swoop down upon me one afternoon at an unsuspecting and innocent literary luncheon in Pasadena's Vista del Arroyo Hotel.

Robert Nathan, I believe, was one of the speakers, along with a number of other authors. I was to have five minutes on the program to read a few poems from my latest collection of folk verses, *Shakespeare in Harlem,* hardly a radical book.

When I arrived at the hotel by car from Los Angeles, I noticed quite a crowd in the streets where the traffic seemed to be tangled. So I got out some distance from the front of the hotel and walked through the grounds to the entrance, requesting my car to return at three o'clock. When I asked in the lobby for the location of the luncheon, I was told to wait until the desk clerk sent for the chairman, George Palmer Putnam. Mr. Putnam arrived with the manager, both visibly excited. They informed me that the followers of Aimee McPherson were vehemently picketing the hotel because of my appearance there. The manager added with an aggrieved look that he could not have such a commotion in front of his hotel. Either I would have to go or he would cancel the entire luncheon.

Mr. Putnam put it up to me. I said that rather than inconvenience several hundred guests and a half dozen authors, I would withdraw—except that I did not know where my car had gone, so would someone be kind enough to drive me to the station. Just then a doorman came in to inform the manager that traffic was completely blocked in front of the hotel. Frantically the manager rushed out. About that time a group of Foursquare Gospel members poured into the lobby in uniforms and armbands and surrounded me and George Palmer Putnam demanding to know if we were Christians. Before I could say anything, Mr. Putnam lit into them angrily, saying it was none of their business and stating that under our Constitution a man could have any religion he chose, as well as freedom to express himself.

Just then an old gentleman about seventy-two who was one of the organizers of the literary luncheon came up, saying he had been asked to drive me to the station and get me out of there so they could start the luncheon. Shaking hands with Mr. Putnam, I accompanied the old gentleman to the street. There Aimee's sound truck had been backed across the roadway blocking all passage so that limousines, trucks, and taxis were tangled up in all directions. The sound truck was playing "God Bless America" while hundreds of pickets milled about with signs denouncing Langston Hughes—atheistic Red.

Rich old ladies on the arms of their chauffeurs were trying to get through the crowd to the luncheon. Reporters were dashing about.

None of the people recognized me, but in the excitement the old gentleman could not find his car. Finally he hailed a taxi and nervously thrust a dollar into the driver's hand with the request that I be driven to the station. He asked to be excused himself in order to get back to the luncheon. Just as I reached out the door to shake hands in farewell, three large white ladies with banners rushed up to the cab. One of them screamed, "We don't shake hands with niggers where we come from!"

The thought came over me that the picketing might turn into a race riot, in which case I did not wish to be caught in a cab in a traffic jam alone. I did not turn loose the old gentleman's hand. Instead of shaking it in farewell, I simply pulled him into the taxi with me, saying, "I thought you were going to the station, too."

As the pickets snarled outside, I slammed the door. The driver started off, but we were caught in the traffic blocked by the sound truck lustily playing "God Bless America." The old gentleman trembled beside me, until finally we got clear of the mob. As we backed down a side street and turned to head for the station, the sirens of approaching police cars were heard in the distance.

Later I learned from the afternoon papers that the whole demonstration had been organized by Aimee McPherson's publicity man, and that when the police arrived he had been arrested for refusing to give up the keys to the sound truck stalled midway the street to block the traffic. This simply proved the point I had tried to make in the poem—that the church might as well bid Christ goodbye if His gospel were left in the hands of such people.

Four years later I was to be picketed again in Detroit by Gerald L. K. Smith's Mothers of America—for ever since the Four-square Gospel demonstration in California, reactionary groups have copied, used and distributed this poem. Always they have been groups like Smith's, never known to help the fight for democratic Negro rights in America, but rather to use their energies to foment riots such as that before Detroit's Sojourner Truth housing project where the Klan-minded tried to prevent colored citizens from occupying government homes built for them.

I have had one threatening communication signed *A Klans-man*. And many scurrilous anonymous anti-Negro letters from persons whose writing did not always indicate illiteracy. On a few occasions, reactionary elements have forced liberal sponsors to cancel their plans to present me in a reading of my poems. I recall that in Gary, Indiana, some years ago the colored teachers were threatened with the loss of their jobs if I accepted their invitation to appear at one of the public schools. In another city a white high school principal, made apprehensive by a small group of reactionary parents, told me that he communicated with the F. B. I. at Washington to find out if I were a member of the Communist party. Assured that I was not, with the approval of his school board, he presented me to his student body. To further fortify his respectability, that morning at assembly, he had invited all of the Negro ministers and civic leaders of the town to sit on the stage in a semi-circle behind me. To the students it must have looked like a kind of modern minstrel show as it was the first time any Negroes at all had been invited to their assembly.

So goes the life of a social poet. I am sure none of these things would ever have happened to me had I limited the subject matter of my poems to roses and moonlight. But, unfortunately, I was born poor—and colored—and almost all the prettiest roses I have seen have been in rich white people's yards—not in mine. That is why I cannot write exclusively about roses and moonlight—for sometimes in the moonlight my brothers see a fiery cross and a circle of Klansmen's hoods. Sometimes in the moonlight a dark body sways from a lynching tree—but for his funeral there are no roses.

Phylon, Fall 1947

LANGSTON HUGHES SPEAKS*

*The following piece is a summary of information offered by Hughes to the Senate Permanent Subcommittee on Investigations of the Committee on Government Operations, March 26, 1953.

During a period in my life coinciding roughly with the beginning of the Scottsboro Case and the depression of the 1930's and running through to the Nazi-Soviet Pact, I wrote a number of poems which reflected my then deep sympathies with certain of the aims and objectives of the leftist philosophies and the interests of the Soviet Union in the problems of poverty, minorities, colonial peoples, and particularly of Negroes and Jim Crow. Most of these poems appeared only in booklet form and have long been out of print. I was amazed to learn that some of these out-dated examples of my work are today being circulated in our State Department's overseas libraries. Written, some of them, partially in leftist terminology with the red flag as a symbol of freedom, they could hardly serve to present a contemporary picture of American ideals or of my personal ones.

I am not now and have never been a member of the Communist party, and have so stated over the years in my speeches and writings. But there is in my family a long history of participation in social struggle—from my grandfather who went to prison for helping slaves to freedom and another relative who died with John Brown at Harper's Ferry to my great uncle, John M. Langston, only Negro Representative in Congress from Virginia following the Reconstruction, and who had supported Abraham Lincoln in his recruiting Negro troops, and spoken for freedom on the same platform with Garrison and Phillips. In my own youth, faced with the problems of both poverty and color, and penniless at the beginning of the depression, I was strongly attracted by some of the promises of Communism, but always with the reservations, among others, of a creative writer wishing to preserve my own freedom of action and expression—and as an American Negro desiring full integration into our body politic. These two reservations, particularly (since I could never accept the totalitarian regimentation of the artist nor the Communist theory of a Negro state for the Black Belt) —were among other reasons why I never contemplated joining the Communist party, although various aspects of Communist interests were for some years reflected in the emotional content of my writing. But I was shocked at the Nazi-Soviet Pact, just as I am shocked now by the reported persecution of the Jewish people. And I was disturbed by the complete lack of freedom of press and publication I observed in the USSR. In our own country I have been greatly heartened in recent years by the progress being made in race-relations, by the recent Supreme Court decisions relative to Negro education, restrictive covenants, the ballot, and travel. My work of the war years, and my latest books have reflected this change of emphasis and development in my own thinking and orientation. This is, I think, clearly and simply shown in the last paragraph of my latest book [*The First Book of Negroes*]:

"Our country has many problems still to solve, but America is young, big, strong, and beautiful. And we are trying very hard to be, as the flag says, 'one nation, indivisible, with liberty and justice for all.' Here people are free to vote and work out their problems. In some countries people are governed by rulers, and ordinary folks can't do a thing about it. But here all of us are a part of democracy. By taking an interest in our government, and by treating our neighbors as we would like to be treated, each one of us can help make our country the most wonderful country in the world."

The Crisis, May 1953